ETHICAL DECISION MAKING IN CLINICAL M

OXFORD WORKSHOP SERIES:

AMERICAN ACADEMY OF CLINICAL NEUROPSYCHOLOGY

Series Editors

Greg J. Lamberty, *Editor-in-Chief*
Ida Sue Baron
Richard Kaplan
Sandra Koffler
Jerry Sweet

Volumes in the Series

Understanding Somatization in the Practice of Clinical Neuropsychology
Greg J. Lamberty

Mild Traumatic Brain Injury and Postconcussion Syndrome
Michael A. McCrea

• AMERICAN ACADEMY OF •
CLINICAL NEUROPSYCHOLOGY

ETHICAL DECISION MAKING
IN CLINICAL NEUROPSYCHOLOGY

Shane S. Bush

OXFORD WORKSHOP SERIES

OXFORD
UNIVERSITY PRESS

2007

OXFORD
UNIVERSITY PRESS

Oxford University Press

Oxford University Press, Inc., publishes works that further
Oxford University's objective of excellence
in research, scholarship, and education.

Oxford   New York
Auckland   Cape Town   Dar es Salaam   Hong Kong   Karachi
Kuala Lumpur   Madrid   Melbourne   Mexico City   Nairobi
New Delhi   Shanghai   Taipei   Toronto

With offices in
Argentina   Austria   Brazil   Chile   Czech Republic   France   Greece
Guatemala   Hungary   Italy   Japan Poland   Portugal   Singapore
South Korea   Switzerland   Thailand   Turkey   Ukraine   Vietnam

Library of Congress Cataloging-in-Publication Data
Bush, Shane S., 1965–
Ethical decision making in clinical neuropsychology / Shane S. Bush.
p. ; cm.—(Oxford workshop series)
Includes bibliographical references.
ISBN 978-0-19-532822-6
1. Clinical neuropsychology—Decision making.   2. Clinical neuropsychology—Moral
and ethical aspects.   I. American Academy of Clinical Neuropsychology.
II. Title.   III. Series.
[DNLM: 1. Ethics, Clinical.   2. Neuropsychology—ethics.
3. Decision Making—ethics. WL 21 B978e 2008]
RC386.6.N48B87 2008
616.8—dc22   2007007073

1 3 5 7 9 8 6 4 2

Printed in the United States of America
on acid-free paper

To Dana, Sarah, and Megan.
I know this much is true.

Preface

The ethical practice of clinical neuropsychology requires an ongoing examination and discussion of both long-standing and evolving practice issues as well as the ethical, legal, and professional resources on which we rely to guide our professional conduct. I feel fortunate to be part of the ongoing examination and discussion process and hope that this book helps advance the process a little further.

This book was written as a companion to a workshop at the 2007 American Academy of Clinical Neuropsychology (AACN) conference in Denver, Colorado. As such, it was intended to be relatively concise, with a focus on select points and issues (described in part I) that are of particular importance, some of which were not addressed in previous neuropsychology ethics texts, and the time frame for completion of this book was relatively brief. Although not meant to be the definitive work on ethical issues in clinical neuropsychology, this book does address many of the issues that are essential for ethical neuropsychological practice, and I hope it will be a useful resource for neuropsychology students, trainees, and practitioners, including those preparing for board certification.

Of course, discussion of ethical dilemmas involves examination of the gray areas in neuropsychology—areas of controversy that by definition preclude universal agreement. As a result, some readers will disagree with points made or positions taken herein. There can be more than one appropriate course of action for any given situation. Well-reasoned, evidence-based disagreement can be channeled into more discussion of ethical and professional issues and perhaps further the evolution of neuropsychology ethics; I hope that such discourse occurs.

As I look back a few years to the time before I began publishing with any regularity, I would have imagined that the more one publishes, the less one needs to rely on assistance from others. However, I can now say emphatically that the more I have published, the more I have relied on colleagues and friends for information, discussions of ethical and professional issues, critical reviews of my ideas and work, sharing of manuscripts, and opportunities for projects such as this one. Without attempting to identify everyone by name,

I hope that the friends and colleagues who have formally or informally interacted with me regarding ethical and professional matters during the past
few years know how much I appreciate their time and consideration.

For this book, I am very grateful to Greg Lamberty and the other members
of the 2007 AACN conference planning committee for inviting me to both
present at the conference and contribute a book as part of the inaugural
collection for the Oxford-published AACN book series. I am also grateful to
the anonymous peer reviewers and senior editor Shelley Reinhardt and assistant editor Abby Gross of Oxford University Press for their kind assistance.

Continuing Education Credit

To access the book's Continuing Education component, visit
http://theaacn.org/ce/book_series

Author's Workshop Materials

To download materials from the author's workshop presentation,
such as PowerPoints, visit
www.oup.com/us/companion.websites/9780195328226

Contents

ETHICAL DECISION MAKING IN CLINICAL NEUROPSYCHOLOGY

PART ONE

INTRODUCTION

The study of brain-behavior relationships and the appropriate clinical application of information obtained through such studies can only be fully realized if sufficient attention is paid to ethical issues. Achieving and maintaining an awareness of common ethical challenges and an understanding of ethics resources allow neuropsychologists to pursue high standards of practice, minimize the potential for ethical conflicts, and appropriately resolve ethical challenges when they occur. But how does a practitioner of a relatively young specialty that is not without controversy determine ethical practice?

The ability to anticipate, avoid, and resolve ethical conflicts in neuropsychology is a dynamic process that must be developed and maintained over time. Ethics codes and professional guidelines are drafted and updated, changes in clinical practice occur, and new laws are implemented. To practice in a manner consistent with the highest ethics principles, neuropsychologists must be able to integrate the evolving ethical and legal requirements into their professional activities. Neuropsychologists should also be able to approach ethical challenges in a systematic manner, which can be facilitated through use of a decision-making model.

Ethical decision making would be much simpler if readily identified "bottom-line" answers existed for all ethics questions. Bottom-line answers describe how to resolve specific ethics questions and can be applied consistently across settings and contexts. For some questions, such as, "Is it appropriate to have sex with my therapy client?" the bottom-line answer is obvious and can be applied consistently. However, more ambiguous variations may emerge, such as, "Is it appropriate to have sex with my attorney client, and does the two-year abstention rule apply even though the case has been settled?" Although bottom-line ethics may be refreshing to an ethics student, the considerable variability of case details renders such an approach insufficient in most situations.

The purposes of this book are to (1) present common ethical challenges in clinical neuropsychology; (2) review ethical requirements, professional guidelines, and other published literature relevant to clinical neuropsychology; (3) provide an ethical decision-making model; (4) describe ethical decision making in neuropsychology from the perspective of positive ethics; and (5) illustrate the application of the American Psychological Association (APA) Ethics Code and the decision-making model through clinical vignettes. Achievement of these goals will build on the scholarly works of colleagues in previous books (Bush, 2005a; Bush & Drexler, 2002). As professional ethics and neuropsychological practice evolve, the application of professional ethics to clinical neuropsychology must also evolve. The present book applies the most recent ethics resources and thinking to clinical neuropsychology.

The book is organized according to the APA Ethics Code (APA, 2002). The APA Ethics Code was selected for the following reasons: (1) it is the primary ethics resource for psychologists; (2) it addresses most of the professional activities in which neuropsychologists engage; (3) it is used by the APA to adjudicate complaints of ethical misconduct; and (4) it has been adopted by many state psychology boards as their definition of acceptable professional conduct. However, as is emphasized throughout this book, there are many ethical, legal, and professional resources that neuropsychologists should consider when engaging in ethical decision making. Despite the evolving and controversial aspects of neuropsychology, practitioners who maintain an awareness of potential ethical challenges, embrace positive ethics, use an ethical decision-making model, and consider all relevant resources will be well positioned to make good ethical decisions.

1

■ ■ ■

Ethical and Legal Resources

Clinical neuropsychologists establish confidence in their conclusions because such conclusions are based, in large part, on objective data and are empirically derived. All necessary resources, including normative data, test manuals, and relevant research, are consulted. In the case of a patient presenting for evaluation with complex neurocognitive and emotional symptoms,[1] it would be unusual to have a neuropsychologist arrive at a diagnostic conclusion without obtaining the necessary information and data and considering the professional literature. However, when considering ethical issues, it is not uncommon for the same data-driven clinicians to begin their conclusions with the words "I think." They might say, "I think the problem is . . ." or "I think you should . . ." Although little empirical information is available to facilitate ethical decision making, many professional resources exist to inform and assist neuropsychologists with the ethical decision-making process.

When considering ethical questions or confronting ethical challenges, most neuropsychologists in the United States naturally seem to first turn to the

---

[1] The terms *patient, client, examinee,* and *consumer* are often used interchangeably in the neuropsychological literature to describe those persons who receive or retain neuropsychological services. In this book, all of these terms are used. *Patient* refers to persons who receive neuropsychological services in clinical contexts. *Client* may refer to the recipient of neuropsychological services or the party (e.g., an attorney) who retains the neuropsychologist. The simple distinction of the payor being the client is not used in this book because an insurance company may pay for services, but that does not make the insurance company the client. *Examinee* refers to one who is undergoing or has undergone a neuropsychological examination (i.e., evaluation); the term is typically used in contexts (e.g., forensic contexts) in which the person being evaluated is not a patient or the retaining party. *Consumer* refers to those persons who seek neuropsychological services for themselves or others. In this book, an attempt is made to use terms that are as specific as possible for a given context, although at times a word or phrase may be used for consistency with the Ethics Code or other resource.

American Psychological Association (APA) Ethics Code (2002), in part because the code is used to adjudicate ethics complaints. Despite the importance of the APA Ethics Code, many ethical, legal, and professional directives and guidelines exist to help neuropsychologists select good courses of action (see table 1.1).

Ethics Codes

The ethics codes of professional organizations are developed to reduce the vagueness inherent in professional values (Beauchamp & Childress, 2001). They provide a common set of principles and standards from which members of the organization or the profession can determine appropriate behaviors. Such codes are typically written broadly to apply to professionals across practice settings and contexts. They establish minimum standards of conduct and serve as the basis of disciplinary actions by professional organizations. The ethics codes may also be adopted in whole or in part by jurisdictional licensing boards to govern the professional activities of practitioners in their jurisdictions. For example, as of 2002, 27 state psychology boards had

Table 1.1 Sources of Ethics-Related Information

1. Ethics codes

2. *Code of Conduct* of the Association of State and Provincial Psychology Boards

3. Jurisdictional laws

4. Publications and position papers of professional organizations

5. International Classification of Functioning, Disability and Health (World Health Organization, 2001)

6. Scholarly works, such as books, articles, and chapters

7. Ethics committees

8. Professional liability insurance carriers

9. Institutional guidelines and resources

10. Colleagues

adopted or followed the APA Ethics Code to govern the professional behavior of psychologists (personal communication, Stephen Behnke, director of the APA Ethics Office, September 12, 2002).

Because professional ethics should apply to all members of the profession, they cannot directly address the ethical nuances experienced by practitioners of specialties. As a result, additional guidelines are produced by members of specialty groups to address ethical questions raised by members of the specialty that are not addressed by the broader code of the discipline. In this section, ethics codes and professional guidelines relevant to the practice of clinical neuropsychology in North America are presented. It is essential that neuropsychologists are familiar with such resources.

APA Ethics Code

The APA Ethics Code provides guidance for ethical psychological practice. The code has as its goal "the welfare and protection of the individuals and groups with whom psychologists work and the education of members, students, and the public regarding ethical standards of the discipline" (Preamble). The code consists of four sections: Introduction and Applicability, Preamble, General Principles, and Ethical Standards.

> The Introduction discusses the intent, organization, procedural considerations, and scope of application of the Ethics Code. The Preamble and General Principles are aspirational goals to guide psychologists toward the highest ideals of psychology. Although the Preamble and General Principles are not themselves enforceable rules, they should be considered by psychologists in arriving at an ethical course of action. The Ethical Standards set forth enforceable rules for conduct as psychologists. Most of the Ethical Standards are written broadly, in order to apply to psychologists in varied roles, although the application of an Ethical Standard may vary depending on the context. The Ethical Standards are not exhaustive.

The five General Principles are beneficence and nonmaleficence, fidelity and responsibility, integrity, justice, and respect for people's rights and dignity. The General Principles are considered aspirational and are intended "to guide and inspire psychologists toward the very highest ethical ideals of the profession." The 10 Ethical Standards are the enforceable minimum level of ethical conduct for psychologists who are APA members or whose state boards for psychology have adopted the APA Ethics Code as the professional regulations or rules of practice for licensed psychologists. The standards and their application to clinical neuropsychology are addressed in detail in part II of this book.

By addressing both standards and principles, the code provides "the mandatory floor or minimum standards adopted by the profession (i.e., remedial ethics)" and encourages "voluntary efforts to live out moral ideals" (Knapp & VandeCreek, 2006, p. 3). The remedial and aspirational components of the code are interactive, with an understanding of each improving the ability of psychologists to practice in a manner consistent with each other.

For neuropsychologists practicing in the United States, the APA Ethics Code is typically the first resource to consider when determining ethical conduct. Although all of the Ethical Standards hold relevance for neuropsychologists, one's practice setting, contexts, and activities determine which standards are of greatest relevance.

CPA Ethics Code

The Canadian Code of Ethics for Psychologists, third edition (Canadian Psychological Association [CPA], 2000) differs from the APA Ethics Code in both format and content, although they share a commitment to a North American "*common morality* or an intuitive sense of what is honest, helpful, trustworthy, or civil" (Knapp & VandeCreek, 2006, p. 15). Through its review of underlying values and responsibilities, the CPA Ethics Code reflects the influence of its philosophical foundation.

The code provides four core ethical principles that were selected in part based on the responses of Canadian psychologists to hypothetical ethical dilemmas sent by the CPA Committee on Ethics during development of the code. Each principle is followed by a description of the values that underlie it, and each values statement is followed by a set of standards that illustrate the application of the principle and values to specific psychological activities.

The code also provides a hierarchical listing, with rationale, of the steps to be taken when its core principles conflict. Because of the acknowledged dilemmas that are inevitably encountered even with such weighting of principles, the CPA code provides a 10-step ethical decision-making model. The code is intended to both guide ethical behavior and serve as the basis for adjudicating ethics complaints. This is an important resource not only for Canadian neuropsychologists but also for all neuropsychologists interested in understanding the values underlying ethical standards and invested in pursuing ethical ideals.

Professional Guidelines

The APA Ethics Code, in the Introduction and Applicability section, acknowledges the value of seeking direction from multiple resources when making decisions about ethical issues.

> In the process of making decisions regarding their professional behavior, psychologists must consider this Ethics Code in addition to applicable laws and psychology board regulations. In applying the Ethics Code to their professional work, psychologists may consider other materials and guidelines that have been adopted or endorsed by scientific and professional psychological organizations and the dictates of their own conscience, as well as consult with others within the field.

ASPPB Code of Conduct

The purpose of the Code of Conduct of the Association of State and Provincial Psychology Boards (ASPPB, 2005) is to provide rules that "constitute the standards against which the required professional conduct of a psychologist is measured." Although the code is enforceable only in those jurisdictions that have adopted it for such purpose, the code provides an additional valuable resource for neuropsychologists seeking clarification regarding ethical behavior.

Standards for Educational and Psychological Testing (SEPT)

The intent of the SEPT (American Educational Research Association, American Psychological Association, & National Council on Measurement in Education, 1999) is "to promote the sound and ethical use of tests and to provide a basis for evaluating the quality of testing practices" (p. 1). Additionally, the purpose of the standards is "to provide criteria for the evaluation of tests, testing practices, and the effects of test use" (p. 2). The SEPT, a 289-page book, is an excellent addition to APA Ethical Standard 9 (Assessment); it provides a more detailed review of assessment-related behaviors found in Ethical Standard 9 and provides clarification of assessment-related behaviors that appear contradictory or incomplete in Ethical Standard 9, such as is encountered in Ethical Standard 9.04, Release of Test Data.

Position Papers of Professional Organizations

Position statements or white papers reflect the general consensus of practitioners of a specialty and offer clarification of details of practice areas that are beyond the scope of an ethics code (see table 1.2 for a list of selected position papers). Many position papers are accessible on the Web sites of the organizations that authored or endorsed them. The National Academy of Neuropsychology (NAN) and the American Academy of Clinical Neuropsychology (AACN) are the primary organizations providing position papers that are specifically relevant to neuropsychologists. Because forensic activities now have a prominent place among the professional activities of neuropsychologists (Sweet, 2005; Sweet et al., 2003a), the Specialty Guidelines for Forensic Psychology (SGFP; Committee on Ethical Guidelines for Forensic Psychologists, 2005 revision) is an essential resource for many neuropsychologists.

Other Published Resources

"Theory and principle are only starting points and general guides for the development of norms of appropriate conduct. They are supplemented by paradigm cases of right action, empirical data, organizational experience, and the like" (Beauchamp & Childress, 2001, p. 2). An emerging readiness for the exchange of ideas and information relevant to ethics in neuropsychology was recognized in the late 1980s and early 1990s (e.g., Ackerman & Banks, 1990; Banja, 1989; Bornstein, 1991; Malec, 1993; Woody, 1989). In 1995, Binder and Thompson published a seminal article that applied the 1992 APA Ethics Code (APA, 1992) to neuropsychological assessment practices. Later that year, Brittain, Frances, and Barth (1995) published the results of a survey regarding ethical issues and dilemmas encountered in neuropsychological practice. These articles signaled an increased emphasis on ethical issues in clinical neuropsychology and were followed by an increasing number of articles, chapters, special journal issues, and books on related topics.

In the past five years or so, there has been a tremendous increase in ethics publications related to neuropsychology, including edited books (Bush, 2005a; Bush & Drexler, 2002), special journal issues (Bush, 2005b; Bush & Martin, 2006a), and a number of other articles and chapters by knowledgeable and experienced clinical neuropsychologists.[2] In addition to publications specific to ethical issues in neuropsychology, general ethics texts address issues of relevance to the field. Similarly, neuropsychology texts address many of the practice issues that are of ethical concern, and some provide specific ethics chapters (e.g., Bush & Martin, 2005a; Grote, 2005). Finally, others with vested interests in appropriate practices, such as private organizations, may generate

---

[2] A list of neuropsychology ethics references compiled in 2004 is posted on the APA Division 40 Web site (div40.org). Appendix B provides an updated list of neuropsychology ethics references.

Ethical Decision Making in Clinical Neuropsychology

Table 1.2 Professional Guidelines Relevant to Neuropsychology

ORGANIZATION	YEAR	TITLE
AACN	1999	Policy on the Use of Non-Doctoral-Level Personnel in Conducting Clinical Neuropsychological Evaluations
	2001	Policy Statement on the Presence of 3rd Party Observers in Neuropsychological Assessments
	2003	Official Position of the American Academy of Clinical Neuropsychology on Ethical Complaints Made Against Clinical Neuropsychologists During Adversarial Proceedings
	2004	Official position of the American Academy of Clinical Neuropsychology on the role of neuropsychologists in the clinical use of fMRI.
AERA, APA, NCME	1999	Standards for Educational and Psychological Testing
AMA	1999	Patient-Physician Relationships in the Context of Work-Related and Independent Medical Examinations
	2000	Peer Review and Medical Expert Witness Testimony
	2004	Expert Witness Testimony
APA	1999	Test Security: Protecting the Integrity of Tests
	2002	Ethical Principles of Psychologists and Code of Conduct
ASPPB	2005	Code of Conduct
CEGFP	1991	Specialty Guidelines for Forensic Psychologists

Table 1.2 (*continued*)

ORGANIZATION	YEAR	TITLE
	2005	Specialty Guidelines for Forensic Psychology (draft)
CPA	2000	Canadian Code of Ethics for Psychologists, 3rd ed.
	2001	Practice Guidelines for Providers of Psychological Services
NAN	2000	Presence of 3rd party Observers During Neuropsychological Testing: Official Statement of the National Academy of Neuropsychology.
	2000	Test Security: Official Position Statement of the National Academy of Neuropsychology
	2000	The Use of Neuropsychology Test Technicians in Clinical Practice: Official Statement of the National Academy of Neuropsychology
	2002	Cognitive Rehabilitation
	2003	Informed Consent: Official Statement of the National Academy of Neuropsychology[a]
	2003	Independent and Court-Ordered Forensic Neuropsychological Examinations: Official Statement of the National Academy of Neuropsychology[b]
	2003	Test Security: An Update. Official Statement of the National Academy of Neuropsychology
	2005	Symptom validity assessment: Practice issues and medical necessity[c]

(*continued*)

Table 1.2 (continued)

ORGANIZATION	YEAR	TITLE
	2006	The importance of neuropsychological assessment for the evaluation of childhood learning disorders[d]
	2006	The use, education, training, and supervision of neuropsychological test technicians (psychometrists) in clinical practice[e]

Notes: AERA: American Educational Research Association; AMA:= American Medical Association
[a]Johnson-Greene & NAN Policy& Planning Committee (2005).
[b]Bush et al. (2005a).
[c]Bush et al. (2005b).
[d]Silver et al. (2006).
[e]Puente et al. (2006).

articles or position statements of interest to neuropsychologists and consumers of neuropsychological services (e.g., Psychological Corporation, 2004).

Bioethical Principles

Principle-based (prima facie) ethics represents a prominent philosophical system widely adopted across health care disciplines. The principles, evident in many professional ethical codes, reflect the foundational values of society. For example, the right to self-determination and the right to live safely are primary values in North America. According to Behnke, Perlin, and Bernstein (2003) ethical dilemmas should be approached by first asking the following questions: "What values are at issue? And how can I act consistent with those values?" (p. 225). Determining the values that underlie ethical or legal requirements helps clarify the spirit behind the letter of the standard or law, thereby clarifying the appropriate courses of action (Behnke, Perlin, & Bernstein, 2003).

The prima facie nature of this multiprinciple system requires that an obligation to one principle be maintained unless it conflicts with an equal or stronger obligation (Beauchamp & Childress, 2001; Knapp & VandeCreek, 2006). When two or more ethical obligations conflict, a neuropsychologist must determine the *actual* obligation by examining the relative weights of all competing prima facie obligations and make a decision that reflects the greatest balance of right over wrong.

Beauchamp and Childress (2001) described four core bioethical principles as being particularly important to biomedical ethics: respect for autonomy, beneficence, nonmaleficence, and justice. These principles are clearly evident in the 2002 APA Ethics Code. Respect for autonomy refers to the right of competent patients to make the decisions that govern their lives, as long as the decisions do not negatively impact the rights of others. Respect for patient autonomy contrasts with the paternalistic approach to decision making traditionally encountered in medicine by which the health care professional is assumed to know what procedures are in a patient's best interests and should be performed. Respect for patient autonomy supports the right of competent, well-informed patients to accept or decline examination or treatment options and be involved in making the decisions that affect their lives. The right of individuals to be informed of the nature of proposed neuropsychological services and, in most clinical situations, accept or decline such services is based on this principle.

The principle of nonmaleficence refers to a moral obligation for clinicians to do no harm. Although the importance of this long-standing tenet is immediately evident, determinations regarding which actions or inactions constitute harm or which individual, organization, or system is owed such an obligation can be difficult to make. *Beneficence* refers to a moral obligation to take action to advance the welfare of others. Beneficence encompasses the promotion of the rights and health of others, as well as defense of the rights of others and the prevention of harm.

Justice refers to "fair, equitable, and appropriate treatment in light of what is due or owed to persons" (Beauchamp & Childress, 2001, p. 226). Justice has two components: distributive justice and formal justice. Distributive justice refers to the equitable distribution of health care resources. Formal justice refers to equal treatment for those who are equals and unequal treatment for those who are not equals. Challenges to the successful application of the principle of justice lie in defining what is equitable and determining which individuals or groups are equals.

Two additional moral principles (fidelity and general beneficence) are also relevant to neuropsychology. Fidelity (Bersoff & Koeppl, 1993; Kitchener, 1984) refers to the obligation to be truthful and faithful, keep promises, and maintain loyalty. General beneficence (Knapp & VandeCreek, 2006) refers to the clinician's responsibility to the public at large (i.e., society).

Legal Considerations

Neuropsychologists must be familiar with the jurisdictional laws that regulate their practices. In the Introduction and Applicability section of the APA Ethics Code, psychologists are advised to consider applicable laws and psychology board regulations as they make decisions regarding ethical conduct. However, whereas state and federal laws provide specific direction for the management of fundamental aspect of psychological practice, more specific activities pertaining to psychological specialty practices (such as neuropsychology) may not be adequately addressed by statutory law. In such instances, review of case law can clarify preferred conduct. Topics such as acceptability of scientific evidence in court (*Daubert v. Merrell Dow Pharmaceuticals*, 1993) and release of raw test data (e.g., *Carpenter v. Superior Court of Alameda County*, 2006; *Detroit Edison Co. v. NLRB*, 1979; *Rompilla v. Beard*, 2005) have been addressed in cases involving psychologists or neuropsychologists.

The Health Insurance Portability and Accountability Act

At the federal level in the United States, the Health Insurance Portability and Accountability Act (HIPAA) took effect in April 2003. The legislation was intended to simplify and protect the confidentiality of electronic billing and transmission of health information and provide increased patient access to their medical records, including the patients' right to amend their medical records to clarify errors. Although those goals may seem logical and straightforward, the legislation evolved into a complex series of administrative rules with exceptions for certain settings and has been a source of confusion and frustration for many practitioners.

Of relevance to neuropsychologists providing services in medicolegal contexts, HIPAA allows that information compiled in anticipation of use in civil, criminal, and administrative proceedings is not subject to the same right of review and amendment as is health care information in general [§164.524(a)(1)(ii)] (U.S. Department of Health and Human Services, 2003). Providing further elaboration, Connell and Koocher (2003) stated that forensic practice may not be subject to HIPAA for the following reasons: (1) forensic services are designed to serve a legal purpose, rather than a therapeutic purpose; (2) forensic services are provided at the request of a party or entity outside the health care system; (3) forensic services fall outside health insurance coverage because they do not constitute health care; (4) forensic psychologists do not ordinarily transmit data electronically, except in the specific ways for which consent has historically been obtained from the litigant; and (5) no new protections or rights accrue to examinees by way of HIPAA compliance (i.e., no new right of access and amendment of information gathered in anticipation of litigation) [§164.524(a) (1)(ii)] (U.S. Department of Health and Human Services, 2003).

In contrast, as noted by Connell and Koocher (2003), some forensic practitioners have argued that HIPAA compliance remains necessary in forensic contexts. This argument is based on the following points: (1) assessment and diagnosis with respect to an individual's mental condition or functional status may in fact constitute health care, rendering psychologists in such contexts covered entities; (2) to obtain health care information about a litigant from other service providers, psychologists must provide assurance that the information will be handled securely; and (3) the question of whether forensic psychologists are covered entities will likely fall to case law for resolution, and it may be preferable to become compliant than to become the case that decides the issue. When HIPAA and state laws conflict, neuropsychologists are advised to adhere to the law that is most protective of healthcare information.

Conflicts Between Ethics and Law

At times, neuropsychologists encounter conflicts between professional ethics and laws. When professional ethics require a higher standard of professional behavior than the law, neuropsychologists should attempt to compromise with legal authorities. The APA Ethics Code states:

> If this Ethics Code establishes a higher standard of conduct than is required by law, psychologists must meet the higher ethical standard. If psychologists' ethical responsibilities conflict with law, regulations, or other governing legal authority, psychologists make known their commitment to this Ethics Code and take steps to resolve the conflict in a responsible manner. If the conflict is unresolvable via such means, psychologists may adhere to the requirements of the law, regulations, or other governing authority in keeping with basic principles of human rights.

Efforts to compromise with legal authorities are often successful for three reasons: (1) the legal system will receive the information or action it needs, (2) the integrity of neuropsychological information or techniques will be preserved, and (3) legal authorities will better understand the ethical concerns of neuropsychologists and the specialty's commitment to high practice standards. When doubts regarding appropriate actions in legal matters persist, it is advisable to seek consultation with one's own legal counsel. Because of the potential to receive a biased response, it is generally not wise to seek such counsel from the retaining attorney involved in the matter.

Colleagues

Colleagues offer a rich and readily available source of information and guidance on ethical matters. Although it is expected that all neuropsychologists have spent some time considering ethical issues, not all colleagues are equally knowledgeable about ethical matters or experienced in the resolution of ethical challenges. As a result, it is advisable to carefully consider which colleagues to consult or carefully weigh the information or guidance obtained from multiple sources.

Consultation with colleagues can occur in three ways. First, neuropsychologists can seek consultation from individual colleagues or informal groups of colleagues, such as via online discussion groups. Colleagues who have confronted similar ethical issues can be particularly valuable sources of information and guidance. Local colleagues offer the potential advantage of having knowledge of both the jurisdictional laws and ethical aspects of the case. However, consulting colleagues in other areas helps preserve privacy and maximizes objectivity when the ethical problem involves another colleague. Establishing consultative relationships with several colleagues can be beneficial and increases the likelihood of expertise regarding specific aspects of practice. Consultations with colleagues may be formalized by establishing a consultation agreement, retaining the colleague as a consultant at an hourly fee, and requesting that the consultant maintain a record of the consultation. If needed later, such consultation can be provided as evidence of one of the attempts made to resolve the ethical challenge in a professional and thoughtful manner (Bush, Connell, & Denney, 2006).

Second, consultation with ethics committees allows neuropsychologists to access the collective knowledge of colleagues representing diverse professional activities. The expertise and diversity associated with committees allow issues to be examined by experts with fresh perspectives, outside the "groupthink process that can affect practitioners of any specialty. Third, professional liability insurance carriers offer consultation to assist practitioners that are confronting complex ethical issues. The advice provided from liability insurance carriers typically comes from a risk management perspective, which can be particularly valuable for avoiding misconduct but may not always be consistent with the pursuit of ethical ideals.

Learning Exercises

1. List the four general bioethical principles described by Beauchamp and Childress.

2. List three to five ethical and professional resources.

3. Describe three laws specific to your practice. Consider any conflicts between legal and ethical requirements.

2

■ ■ ■

Positive Ethics

In the tradition of remedial ethics, "disciplinary codes represent only the ethical 'floor' or minimum standards to which psychologists should adhere" (Knapp & VandeCreek, 2006, p. 9). "Ethics should focus not only on how a few psychologists harm patients but also on how all psychologists can do better at helping them" (Knapp & VandeCreek, 2006, p. 10). Positive ethics represents a shift away from remedial ethics to a voluntary commitment to pursuing ethical ideals, motivated by deeply held moral principles. Rather than neuropsychologists simply doing the minimum that is necessary to avoid accusations of ethical misconduct, a positive ethics approach emphasizes the importance of aspiring to the highest principles of ethical practice. Positive ethics is proactive, requiring practitioners to take steps to promote exemplary behavior throughout their professional activities and careers, not just when faced with ethical challenges.

When considering ethical issues, "the question that should be asked is not, What must I do to fulfill the minimum requirements of the APA Ethics Code? Instead, it should be, What must I do to fulfill my ethical ideals? If psychologists strive to become moral maximalists, instead of moral minimalists, they will still follow the disciplinary codes but only as the beginning of their ethical responsibilities" (Knapp & VandeCreek, 2006, p. 25). Additionally, "if we expect only the moral minimum, we have lost an ennobling sense of excellence in character and performance" (Beauchamp & Childress, 2001, p. 44).

Positive ethics also encourages practitioners to integrate their personal ideals with their professional lives (Knapp & VandeCreek, 2006). Although most members of a society share common values, individuals vary in the extent to which they embrace different values. Unique life experiences, cultural background, religious beliefs, and other factors influence the kinds of personal values that guide decisions. Practitioners who perceive a connection between their personal values and the values underlying professional ethics will show more commitment to their professional ethics than those practitioners who do not have such a connection.

Pursuit of ethical ideals typically requires additional time and expense than is required by minimum enforceable ethical standards, contributing to some clinicians electing not to pursue such ideals. However, time and expense requirements are inadequate excuses for failing to pursue high standards of ethical practice.

Ethical Issues in Clinical Neuropsychology

Although most ethical principles and standards are applicable to clinical neuropsychology, a study that involved collecting ethically challenging vignettes from American Board of Clinical Neurophysiology (ABCN) diplomates revealed that the majority of dilemmas involved boundaries of competence, appropriate use of assessments, and interpretation of assessment results (Brittain, Frances, & Barth, 1995). These ethical priorities for neuropsychologists differ from those of psychologists in general. Pope and Vetter (1992) asked a random sample of American Psychological Association (APA) members about major ethical dilemmas they encountered in their daily work. The three most frequently cited dilemmas were confidentiality; blurred, dual, or conflictual relationships; and payment issues. Forensic issues were fifth, assessment issues were ninth, and competence was eleventh.

In a recent interview of a panel of neuropsychologists with considerable experience addressing ethical issues, the primary challenges that the panelist identified centered around professional competence, increasing involvement of neuropsychologists in forensic activities, and apparent misconduct of colleagues (Bush et al., 2007). I concur that most ethical challenges faced by neuropsychologists in some way involve professional competence and forensic activities. Based on my own professional experiences and familiarity with the literature, I have provided a list of 12 common sources of ethical conflict in clinical neuropsychology (see table 2.1). Professional competence, as the foundations for all practice-related activities, tops the list, and many of the subsequent aspects of practice are related to forensic activities. However, because of the diverse contexts in which neuropsychologists practice and the varied services provided, common sources of ethical conflict will vary.

Although professional competence is essential for ethical practice, competence is not universal; that is, professional competence in certain aspects of

Table 2.1 Common Sources of Ethical Conflict in Clinical Neuropsychology

1. Professional competence

2. Roles and relationships—dual/multiple

3. Test security/release of raw test data

4. Third-party observers

5. Confidentiality

6. Assessment

7. Conflicts between ethics and law

8. False or deceptive statements

9. Objectivity

10. Cooperation with other professionals

11. Informed consent/third-party requests for services

12. Recordkeeping and fees

---

clinical neuropsychology does not imply competence in other areas, nor does it imply that competence in a given aspect of practice will be maintained over time. Formal peer review of one's work increases the likelihood that competent services are being provided. Although board certification is not required for psychological specialties, successful completion of a reasonably rigorous board certification process provides the clearest evidence of competence in neuropsychology. Continuing education in both ethics and clinical aspects of practice is needed to maintain professional competence.

Many authors have examined ethical issues in forensic neuropsychology in recent years (for reviews, see Sweet, Grote, & van Gorp, 2002; the special issue of the *Journal of Forensic Neuropsychology*, Bush, 2005c; the special issue of *Applied Neuropsychology*, Bush & Martin, 2006b). The adversarial nature of the legal system, considerable incentives for biased methods and opinions, and limited training in forensic activities for most clinical neuropsychologists are a formula for ethical misconduct. With increasing involvement of neuropsychologists in forensic activities (Sweet, 2005; Sweet et al., 2003), it is likely that many ethical challenges in this field will continue to be related to forensic aspects of practice.

Although it is important to attempt to address the issues, principles, and standards individually, ethical challenges rarely involve just one principle or standard (Koocher & Keith-Speigel, 1998). Neuropsychologists should strive to understand both the obvious and subtle ethical aspects of their practices, as well as the practices of colleagues.

Learning Exercises

1. What is a primary goal of positive ethics?

2. With regard to positive ethics, what is a primary responsibility and obligation of all practitioners?

3. Describe three ethical challenges commonly encountered in your practice setting.

4. Describe two additional ethical challenges that, although not commonly encountered, may arise in your practice setting.

3

An Ethical Decision-Making Model

Ethical issues become dilemmas for the following reasons: (1) they pit ethical, legal, or organizational requirements against each other; (2) the Ethics Code or laws are silent on the issue; or (3) they require the professional to use judgment. Because ethical dilemmas are complex, the preferred solutions are often difficult to discern. In addition, given the number and variety of resources that are available to assist neuropsychologists with ethical decision making, finding occasional inconsistencies among resources is understandable. To determine a preferred course of action from among conflicting directives and guidelines, practitioners benefit from use of a decision-making model that allows them to weigh the relative importance of the information obtained.

A structured method of information collection and review can facilitate the ethical decision-making process. A number of models have been proposed for clarifying one's own options and the actions of colleagues (Canadian Psychological Association, 1991; Haas & Malouf, 2002; Kitchener, 2000; Koocher & Keith-Spiegel, 1998). Knapp and VandeCreek (2003) reviewed these models and identified five common steps: (1) identification of the problem, (2) development of alternatives, (3) evaluation of alternatives, (4) implementation of the best option, and (5) evaluation of the results. Knapp and VandeCreek (2003) also noted that the models reviewed did not adequately consider emotional and situational factors or the possible need for an immediate response.

The eight-step ethical decision-making model adopted herein was originally proposed by Bush, Connell, and Denney (2006) for application in forensic psychology (see table 3.1). However, the model has also been recommended

TABLE 3.1 ETHICAL DECISION-MAKING MODEL

1. Identify the problem(s) or dilemma(s)

2. Consider the significance of the context and setting

3. Identify and utilize ethical and legal resources

4. Consider personal beliefs and values

5. Develop possible solutions to the problem

6. Consider the potential consequences of various solutions

7. Choose and implement a course of action

8. Assess the outcome and implement changes as needed

Source: Based on the model proposed by Bush, Connell, and Denney (2006)

for use by neuropsychologists (Bush, 2005b; Bush & Martin, 2006a). The model incorporates the five common steps reviewed by Knapp and Vande-Creek (2003a) and integrates the decision-making components that were found to be lacking in those models. Application of this model may assist practitioners in both avoiding ethical misconduct and pursuing ethical ideals. The model consists of the following steps.

Identify the Problem(s) or Dilemma(s)

When faced with complex professional situations, the specific ethical issues are not always easily identified. You may encounter clinical or forensic situations in which something does not seem right, but the origin of the unsettling feeling is unknown. Alternatively, the problems may be readily apparent but may not be of an ethical nature per se. It is often necessary to distinguish between ethical, legal, moral, and professional issues. These overlapping concepts must be clarified to understand the ethical problem or dilemma. It is advisable to remember that consensus is lacking regarding aspects of professional neuropsychological activities, and differing courses of action or opinions may be appropriate in any given context.

Consider the Significance of the Setting and Context

Neuropsychologists provide services and consult in a variety of settings and contexts. In each setting, there are obligations to individuals and institutions. Generally, neuropsychologists have an obligation to provide competent services that advance the welfare of the individuals and institutions to which these obligations are owed without bringing unjust harm to others. You may have obligations to a variety of individuals and institutions, such as referral sources, clients, examinees or patients, guardians or health care proxies, employing institutions, triers of fact, courts, legal systems, the profession of psychology, and society at large.

Some of the obligations to clients and other parties remain consistent, whereas others vary across contexts. The most obvious differences in obligations exist between clinical and forensic contexts (Bush et al., 2005a). For example, neuropsychologists have a general responsibility to avoid causing unjust harm to those with whom they interact professionally, whereas neuropsychological opinions rendered in litigated cases may directly contribute to determinations that are considered harmful to one or more parties. Although these determinations may be harmful to a person's financial future, freedom, or emotional state, such harm, if resulting from competent services, would not be considered unjust.

In addition to differences between clinical and forensic contexts, differences in obligations exist within various clinical and forensic contexts. That is, professional activities that are appropriate in one setting or context may be inappropriate in others. As a result, some professional guidelines that are relevant in one setting or context may be less relevant or completely inapplicable in other situations. For example, evaluation methods that are appropriate in sports concussion contexts would not be considered adequate for use with elderly individuals presenting with symptoms of mild cognitive impairment or for children presenting with possible learning disorders.

Identify and Utilize Ethical and Legal Resources

As previously described, numerous resources exist to aid neuropsychologists in ethical decision making. When a convergence of evidence from multiple sources provides direction for ethical behavior, the course of action is clear. However, the direction suggested by these resources is not always consistent. Not only can ethics resources conflict with each other, but conflicting ethical obligations can be encountered within the same ethics code or set of principles. Despite the conflicts between and within guidelines, reliance on published and interpersonal resources allows neuropsychologists to make good decisions when determining courses of action.

Consider Personal Beliefs and Values

Although the collective values of a society influence professional ethics, individual neuropsychologists endorse different values to varying degrees. Practitioners have a responsibility to assess the extent to which their personal morality is consistent with that of larger society, the profession, and the institutions with which they are involved. Practitioners should also strive to understand their own biases and the potential impact that their values and biases can have on their professional and ethical decision making.

Develop Possible Solutions to the Problem

Positive ethics are action-oriented. That is, positive ethics promotes proactive solutions to potential ethical challenges and appropriate resolution of dilemmas when encountered. Although complex dilemmas may tax even the most thoughtful practitioner, inaction is typically not an acceptable ethical option. Based on the clarification and information obtained in the first four steps of the decision-making model, the practitioner should generate a detailed list of possible solutions.

Consider Potential Consequences

After a list of possible solutions has been generated, the possible positive and negative consequences of each option must be considered. The relative significance of each consequence may need to be weighed. The consequences of a given course of action may extend beyond ethical implications to affect employment, business, and other implications. "What constitutes a reasonable action depends on the circumstances and the options available" (Knapp & VandeCreek, 2006, p. 41). Having considered the potential consequences and their implications, neuropsychologists are advised to choose the option most consistent with ethical ideals.

Choose and Implement a Course of Action

Once potential solutions have been examined and consequences considered, the practitioner must select and, when required, implement the most appropriate course of action. The timing of the action may depend on the ethical issues involved and the context. For example, except for egregious violations, it is typically best to wait for the conclusion of cases in litigation contexts before addressing ethical concerns with colleagues or filing ethics complaints (American Academy of Clinical Neuropsychology, 2003). Consultation with colleagues may be particularly valuable when considering the best time to respond to situations in which timing is an issue.

Assess the Outcome and Implement Changes as Needed

As with the decision-making process, it is advisable to be proactive in assessing the outcome of one's choices and taking steps to modify actions as needed. Following up with the outcomes of anticipated or encountered ethical challenges allows practitioners to modify or readdress decisions or actions in the case if needed and to assess the appropriateness of the decision for future cases. In addition, going through the process and assessing the outcome provide valuable experience that can be shared with students or colleagues to assist them in similar situations.

Documentation

Throughout the ethical decision-making process, it is important to document the efforts made and the steps taken to determine the most appropriate course of action. Such documentation can help others structure their approach to the decision-making process, clarify options, facilitate reasoning, and avoid redundant efforts. Additionally, and perhaps more important in some contexts, having documentation of one's ethical decision-making efforts is essential if evidence of these efforts is later requested during an investigation.

Documentation that follows the outline of the ethical decision-making model presented in table 3.1 and includes the details of the specific situation would likely meet the requirements of most interested parties. Descriptions of the resources consulted, including colleagues and ethics committees, and the underlying reasoning for one's choice of action are particularly valuable. In addition to promoting and demonstrating appropriate action in a given situation, documentation of ethical decision making can facilitate future problem solving in similar cases and serve as a valuable resource for colleagues confronting similar challenges. Maintaining records of how a certain type of ethical challenge is approached, such as responding to requests for raw test data from nonpsychologists, can help ease the decision-making challenge, stress, and time requirements associated with situations that are likely to be encountered again in a certain type of practice.

The following case study vignette demonstrates the application of the ethical decision-making model.

CASE 3.1

Dr. A, a neuropsychologist in independent practice, receives a referral to evaluate a 68-year-old woman who sustained a left middle cerebral artery infarction 6 months ago. The referral is from the patient's neurologist to "rule out dementia and depression" so that appropriate medications can be prescribed. During the initial interview, Dr. A finds that the patient's receptive language is adequate for the clinical interview, based on her ability to follow multistep instructions and respond appropriately to yes/no questions. However, he also found her to have severe expressive language deficits and a dense right hemiparesis. Dr. A wonders whether empirical evidence exists to support his use of traditional neuropsychological tests with patients who have such impaired expressive language skills and are unable to use their dominant hand. He considers the professional and ethical implications of accepting this referral and wonders what he should do.

Identify the Problem(s) or Dilemma(s)

Dr. A has been asked to evaluate a patient and address referral questions for which little empirical evidence exists to support his usual tests. In addition, although Dr. A frequently performs evaluations for the purpose of diagnosing dementias and mood disorders, for many years he has not evaluated patients who sustained severe strokes. Most of the tests he typically uses were not normed with individuals who have severe expressive aphasia or hemiparesis involving the dominant hand. Furthermore, because of the patient's aphasia and hemiparesis, administration of the tests will need to be modified. The extent to which the results obtained from this patient will accurately represent her neurocognitive functioning and psychological state, (given the necessary modifications to test administrations and lack of appropriate norms) is extremely limited. As a result, any recommendations Dr. A could make to the neurologist may result in inappropriate decisions regarding medication. In contrast to these drawbacks, Dr. A may be better able than the neurologist to assess this patient's neurocognitive functioning and emotional state, even with the limitations imposed on standardized testing, thereby resulting in more accurate diagnoses and better medication choices.

Consider the Significance of the Context and Setting

Compared to some institutional practice settings, Dr. A does not have ready access to other health care professionals who may be able to provide helpful consultation. Also, compared to inpatient settings, the ability to provide ongoing monitoring of the patient to further clarify diagnostic impressions and the effects of medical trials is limited.

Identify and Utilize Ethical and Legal Resources

Dr. A identifies the following primary resources for this case:

1. APA Ethics Code
2. Standards for Educational and Psychological Testing (SEPT)
3. Americans with Disabilities Act
4. Chapter on test accommodations in geriatric neuropsychology by Caplan and Shechter (2005)
5. Colleagues, including the APA Division of Neuropsychology ethics subcommittee

The patient has a moral, ethical, and legal right to receive an appropriate neuropsychological evaluation (Americans with Disabilities Act, 1990, General Principle D, Justice), although determining the methods and procedures that constitute an "appropriate" evaluation can be challenging. As stated in the SEPT (1999), "A major issue when testing individuals with disabilities concerns the use of accommodations, modifications, or adaptations. The purpose of these accommodations or modifications is to minimize the impact of test-taker attributes that are not relevant to the construct that is the primary focus of the assessment" (p. 101). To arrive at conclusions that are beneficial and not harmful to the patient, Dr. A has a responsibility to use the most appropriate tests and normative data available, either from test manuals or journal articles, and base his opinions on information sufficient to substantiate the opinions (GP A, Beneficence and Nonmaleficence; ES 2.04, Bases for Scientific and Professional Judgments; ES 9.01, Bases for Assessments; ES 9.06, Interpreting Assessment Results). Dr. A must also consider the empirical support for any adaptations he may make to test administration, tempering his conclusions as needed.

Ethical Standard 9.02, Use of Assessments

(a) Psychologists administer, adapt, score, interpret, or use assessment techniques, interviews, tests, or instruments in a manner and for purposes that are appropriate in light of the research on or evidence of the usefulness and proper application of the techniques.

(b) Psychologists use assessment instruments whose validity and reliability have been established for use with members of the population tested. When such validity or reliability has not been established, psychologists describe the strengths and limitations of test results and interpretation.

SEPT Standard 10.1

In testing individuals with disabilities, test developers, test administrators, and test users should take steps to ensure that the test score inferences accurately reflect the intended construct rather than any disabilities and their associated characteristics extraneous to the intent of the measurement.

Having paid due attention to the needed test accommodations and the potential limits to interpretations, Dr. A must consider whether he is sufficiently familiar with the relevant literature (see Caplan & Shechter, 2005, for a recent review) and has the requisite experience to competently perform the needed modifications and arrive at appropriate conclusions (ES 2.01, Boundaries of Competence; SEPT Standard 12.1).

SEPT Standard 10.1

People who make decisions about accommodations and test modification for individuals with disabilities should be knowledgeable of existing research on the effects of the disabilities in question on test performance. Those who modify tests should also have access to psychometric expertise for doing so.

As van Gorp (2005) stated, "Knowing our limitations is sometimes as or more important than knowing what our science can offer" (p. 212). Dr. A must also keep in mind that "in testing individuals with disabilities for diagnostic and intervention purposes, the test should not be used as the sole indicator of the test taker's functioning. Instead, multiple sources of information should be used" (SEPT Standard 10.12). If Dr. A determines that it is appropriate for him to proceed with the evaluation, he must present the foreseeable benefits and risks of the evaluation to the patient and her legal representative, if someone other than the patient has medical decision-making authority (ES 3.10, Informed Consent; ES 9.03, Informed Consent in Assessments; Johnson-Green & the NAN Policy & Planning Committee, 2005; SEPT Standard 8.4).

Consider Personal Beliefs and Values
Dr. A's beliefs and values are consistent with those represented in the re-sources reviewed. He embraces the right of the patient to receive an appro-priate neuropsychological evaluation, as well as her right to decide whether to pursue an evaluation given the inherent limitations. He questions if he can competently perform an evaluation with the required accommodations and derive accurate conclusions based on the information obtained from such an evaluation.

Develop Possible Solutions to the Problem
Dr. A considers the following four possible solutions.

1. Conduct the evaluation to the best of his ability, explaining to all parties the limitations associated with the conclusions.
2. Conduct the evaluation after arranging for consultation with a colleague who commonly evaluates patients who have sustained severe strokes.
3. Do not perform the evaluation. Inform the neurologist and the patient that neuropsychological evaluation is of little value with such patients.
4. Refer the patient to a neuropsychologist who has more ex-perience with this patient population.

Consider the Potential Consequences of Various Solutions

1. Performing the evaluation may provide helpful information regarding the patient's neuropsychological functioning and diagnosis; however, the potential for misinterpretation of the findings, given Dr. A's limited experience with this population, may be harmful to the patient.

2. Conducting the evaluation with appropriate consultation may allow for proper conclusions to be drawn about the constructs of interest and provide an opportunity for Dr. A to improve his ability to work with stroke patients. However, the likelihood of generating accurate inferences exists with more experienced practitioners.

3. Deciding not to perform the evaluation and informing the patient and the neurologist that such evaluations are not beneficial in such cases may deprive the patient (and future patients) of potentially valuable services.

4. Referring the patient to a neuropsychologist with more recent experience with stroke patients and more familiarity with the relevant literature would allow the patient to get services she needs and provide the neurologist with the information he needs to make an appropriate decision regarding medication. Making such a referral may decrease future referrals from this neurologist, or it may demonstrate integrity and reinforce the neurologist's positive opinion of Dr. A. Dr. A determines that a qualified neuropsychologist is available through a local hospital-based outpatient rehabilitation program.

Choose and Implement a Course of Action

Dr. A chooses the fourth option and refers the patient to his colleague in the outpatient rehabilitation program. Had there not been a qualified colleague nearby, he would have chosen the second option. He explains to the patient and the neurologist that it is in the patient's interest to have the evaluation performed by a neuropsychologist who specializes in working with individuals who have sustained severe strokes. Dr. A contacts the other neuropsychologist and facilitates the referral.

Assess the Outcome and Implement Changes as Needed
The patient receives the most appropriate evaluation possible, although the confidence placed in some of the conclusions remained limited by the required test accommodations.

Learning Exercise

1. Describe two ethical challenges in your work setting(s) and use the decision-making model to resolve the challenges. Write out the steps.

PART TWO

APA ETHICAL STANDARDS APPLIED TO CLINICAL NEUROPSYCHOLOGY

Although many ethical, legal, and professional resources exist to promote appropriate professional conduct, this part focuses on the American Psychological Association (APA) Ethical Standards for two reasons. First, the Ethics Code of the APA is the primary ethical authority for neuropsychologists in the United States, and the code's Ethical Standards are the primary enforceable document for ethical conduct. Second, because this book was written specifically to accompany a workshop at the 2007 American Academy of Clinical Neuropsychologists (AACN) conference and is part of the AACN book series, the emphasis on the Ethical Standards parallels the focus of the ethics component of the American Board of Clinical Neurophysiology (ABCN) oral examination (McSweeny, 2002).

For these reasons, part II presents the application of the Ethical Standards to clinical neuropsychology. The sections of the APA Ethical Standards cited in the following chapters were considered most applicable to clinical neuropsychology and are *not* a complete reproduction of the Ethical Standards. Readers are encouraged to refer to the complete APA Ethics Code for a listing of the Ethical Standards in their entirety. Although only the Ethical Standards are emphasized in this part, the importance of accessing multiple ethical and legal resources during ethical decision making cannot be overstated.

In the 2002 version of the APA Ethics Code, the standard previously devoted to forensic activities was omitted, with some of the information dispersed throughout the code. As a result, this text does not have a separate section on ethical issues related to forensic neuropsychological activities. As with the Ethics Code, some aspects of forensic practice are addressed in relation to specific standards, such as Human Relations, and because of the importance of forensic issues in neuropsychological ethics, an effort was made to include case vignettes of a forensic nature. Nevertheless, neuropsychologists who engage in forensic activities or whose clinical services may interface with the legal system in the future are encouraged to review previous publications of relevance to forensic neuropsychology (see Appendix B).

With the exception of the complex case presented in chapter 13, the ethical decision-making model is not applied to the cases presented in part II. In addition to completing the learning exercises presented at the end of each chapter, readers are encouraged to apply the decision-making model to cases that are particularly challenging or modify the cases so that solutions are not as readily apparent and application of the decision-making model is needed.

4

■ ■ ■

Professional Competence

Professional competence is the foundation of ethical practice. Without the knowledge and skills needed to appropriately address referral questions and serve consumers of neuropsychological services, the remaining ethical requirements are largely irrelevant. Put more plainly, if we do not know what we are doing, we should not be engaging in professional activities. For example, in the absence of competence to provide neuropsychological services, issues such as test selection, informed consent, and confidentiality should not come into play because we should not be engaging in neuropsychological activities in the first place. Conversely, practicing in accordance with other ethical standards is essential for competence. For example, one must understand and apply appropriate methods of test selection, informed consent, and confidentiality to provide competent services. Although this issue is straightforward when considered in the abstract as the dichotomous competence versus incompetence, in most clinical situations the required knowledge and skill set needed to provide a specific service in a certain context is not always obvious.

CASE 4.1

A board-certified neuropsychologist with years of experience evaluating and treating adults with traumatic brain injuries in rehabilitation and forensic settings finds the potential marketing value of work with regional teen sports programs appealing. He arranges with local junior high school and high school football programs to provide comprehensive neuropsychological evaluations of concussed athletes for the purpose of making return-to-play decisions.

■ ■ ■

Ethical Standard 2.01, Boundaries of Competence

(a) Psychologists provide services, teach, and conduct research with populations and in areas only within the boundaries of their competence, based on their education, training, supervised experience, consultation, study, or professional experience. . . .

(e) In those emerging areas in which generally recognized standards for preparatory training do not yet exist, psychologists nevertheless take reasonable steps to ensure the competence of their work and to protect clients/patients, students, supervisees, research participants, organizational clients, and others from harm.

The neuropsychologist in this case previously demonstrated competence in neuropsychology through a formal peer review process. However, board certification does not imply competence in all practice contexts, nor does it imply that competence has been maintained over time. Additionally, although awareness of ethical issues is a requirement for board certification, such certification does imply that ethical conduct is maintained in daily practice. Although still a relatively new subspecialty, sports neuropsychology has developed considerably in recent years, with relatively standard protocols, methods, and guidelines available for clinicians (Echemendia, 2006). Also, ethical issues relevant to sports neuropsychology have been described (Parker, Echemendia, & Milhouse, 2004). By transitioning into a related but new area of practice, the neuropsychologist in this case is practicing outside of his areas of competence.

In addition to lacking familiarity with the state-of-the-art methods and procedures employed in sports neuropsychology, this practitioner lacks experience with adolescents. Ethical Standard 2.01(b) states,

Where scientific or professional knowledge in the discipline of psychology establishes that an understanding of factors associated with age . . . is essential for effective implementation of their

Ethical Decision Making in Clinical Neuropsychology

services or research, psychologists have or obtain the training, experience, consultation, or supervision necessary to ensure the competence of their services.

Neuropsychologists must establish competence with the populations evaluated or treated. In addition to factors like age, neuropsychologists should understand factors associated with gender, gender identity, race, ethnicity, culture, national origin, religion, sexual orientation, disability, language, and socioeconomic status (Ethical Standard 2.01b), all of which may impact his or her actions and clinical opinions.

The importance of professional competence is based on the underlying bioethical principles of beneficence and nonmaleficence. Neuropsychologists have an obligation to benefit (without harming) recipients of their services. Attempting to provide services without having the necessary knowledge base and skill set cannot offer a benefit to recipients of neuropsychological service, and they will likely be harmed. Knapp and VandeCreek (2006) described competence as a three-part process consisting of technical knowledge, social skills, and emotional well-being. Although technical knowledge and social skills are obvious requirements, the ability to withstand emotional challenges associated with difficult clients and the ability to experience and convey positive emotions related to good interpersonal relationships, such as compassion and empathy, are also key (Knapp & VandeCreek, 2006; Pope & Brown, 1996).

In the past, many diverse paths have led to competence in neuropsychology. As clinical neuropsychology has evolved, so have the expectations for appropriate education, training, and experience. The National Academy of Neuropsychology (2001) and the APA Division of Neuropsychology (1989) provide definitions of a neuropsychologist that list minimum education, training, experience, and credentialing requirements. Having met the requirements of these definitions, determination of professional competence is best made through the formal peer review that occurs in the board certification process. With formal peer review, objective professional peers are provided an adequate sample of a candidate's knowledge and abilities and make a determination regarding competence. Objective external feedback, formal or informal, is of critical importance when assuming new professional responsibilities and expanding areas of competence. However, professional competence in new areas of practice is best established in advance by proactively pursuing the knowledge and skills needed to successfully perform the new activities.

A neuropsychologist graduated from a clinical psychology doctoral program with a specialization in neuropsychology. After completing a two-year postdoctoral residency in neuropsychology, she accepted a staff position in a prestigious teaching hospital. She gradually transitioned to part-time private practice over the following five years. She became very busy in her private practice and personal life and did not have time to attend conferences or maintain an affiliation with the teaching hospital. Now, 10 years after completing her postdoc, the families of some of her patients are questioning her conclusions based on information that they found on the Internet, and her forensic work is being strongly criticized by opposing experts, with frequent comments that her results cannot be considered valid.

Ethical Standard 2.03, Maintaining Competence

Psychologists undertake ongoing efforts to develop and maintain their competence.

In some important ways, this neuropsychologist was left behind by advances in the field. Although she was invested in providing competent services and maintaining her knowledge base and skill set, she did not keep up with research and other developments. The ten years passed quickly, and before she knew it, she was faced with the fact that she lacked important information related to her profession. She quickly joined a neuropsychological online discussion list, enrolled in an online neuroanatomy course, joined and attended monthly meetings of a local neuropsychological association, and made plans to attend annual conferences.

Although parameters exist for developing and demonstrating competence in neuropsychological practice, predetermined steps for establishing competence in neuropsychological research and teaching are lacking, as they are in psychology in general (Knapp & VandeCreek, 2006). The institutions that employ teachers and researchers maintain primary oversight of their qualifications and performance. However, motivations or pressures may lead neuropsychologists to assume professional responsibilities that are weakly linked to their formal academic training and for which they are inadequately prepared. A personal investment in limiting one's activities to those for which one is educated and trained is needed until competence in new areas of interest can be pursued. As with clinical activities, peer review of professional activities tends to provide the best method of ensuring competence work.

CASE 4.3

A very experienced and highly credentialed neuropsychologist evaluates and treats litigants with mild traumatic brain injuries sustained in motor vehicle accidents or work-related accidents. He commonly concludes that severe neurocognitive deficits and total and permanent disability more than six months postinjury are causally related to neurological trauma sustained in the accidents. He frequently states that he can determine deficits and disability better than independent examiners because he has interacted with the patients for a much longer period of time.

■ ■ ■

Ethical Standard 2.04, Bases for Scientific and Professional Judgments

Psychologists' work is based upon established scientific and professional knowledge of the discipline.

The neuropsychologist's conclusions in this case are inconsistent with a preponderance of scientific evidence (Larrabee, 2005), and he has a mistaken belief that his impressions and observations over time carry more weight than objective, actuarially based neuropsychological evidence interpreted based on generally established scientific and professional knowledge of the discipline.

For senior clinicians in particular, failure to meet the requirements of this ethical standard may reflect a failure to remain abreast of scientific advances

(Ethical Standard 2.03, Maintaining Competence). Persistent use of outdated methods, procedures, impressions, and judgments is inconsistent with ethical conduct and can become a source of contention in both clinical and forensic contexts. For competent clinicians who remain abreast of scientific and professional advances and still fail to meet the requirements of this ethical standard, especially in forensic contexts, the possibility of intentional bias must be considered. In either case, consumers of neuropsychological services and the reputation of the profession suffer.

In addition to competence in neuropsychological science, neuropsychologists must achieve and maintain competence in neuropsychological ethics. As stated in Bush et al. (2007), achieving and maintaining competence in neuropsychological ethics requires three components:

> 1) obtaining a solid grounding in ethical reasoning that is best acquired through integrated predoctoral and postdoctoral experiences involving didactics and supervised practice allowing for reasonable ethical problem solving capacity, 2) a high level of professional integrity including awareness of one's own limitations and acceptance of the need for consultation with peers, and 3) ongoing education to identify and appropriately manage emerging ethical issues pertaining to psychology in general and within neuropsychology specifically.

Thus, achieving and maintaining competence in neuropsychological ethics is a dynamic process that begins during predoctoral education and training and continues throughout the professional life cycle.

Learning Exercises

1. **List three ways that neuropsychologists can maintain professional competence following completion of postdoctoral training and licensure.**

2. **What is the best way to determine professional competence in clinical, teaching, and research activities?**

5

Human Relations

If professional competence is the foundation of ethical practice, human relations are the cornerstone. Interactions with referral sources, recipients of neuropsychological services, payors, institutions, and others determine whether services are provided and their nature. Professional interactions should be based on appreciation of the interests and obligations of the other parties; respect for individual autonomy, dignity, and differences; and a commitment to one's professional ethics. Professional relationships should be free of unfair discrimination and harassment based on age, gender, gender identity, race, ethnicity, culture, national origin, religion, sexual orientation, disability, socioeconomic status, or any other basis proscribed by law (Ethical Standards 3.01, Unfair Discrimination, and 3.03, Other Harassment). Establishing the boundaries of professional relationships allows neuropsychologists to provide structure and set limits, which are needed to benefit others and minimize the potential for harm.

"The nature of the relationship between the psychologist and the examinee, and the manner in which the relationship is established, have significant implications for the validity of the information that is obtained" (Bush, Connell, & Denney, 2006, p. 60). Professional roles should be established and clarified with all parties at the outset of the relationship, with reminders and additional delineation provided periodically if needed. It is typically advantageous for all parties to establish the parameters of professional relationships in writing. Such documentation helps remind all parties of the original, mutually agreed-on roles and responsibilities.

A young man is referred to a neuropsychologist by his neurologist for evaluation and treatment following a motor vehicle accident. The neuropsychologist performs the evaluation and begins treatment, at which point she receives a request from the patient's attorney for copies of her reports and notes. After one year of treatment, the neuropsychologist determines that a second neuropsychological evaluation is needed to assess progress since the initial evaluation and to update her treatment plan. She conducts the second evaluation and modifies the treatment plan to address persisting deficits.

Ethical Standard 3.05, Multiple Relationships

(a) A multiple relationship occurs when a psychologist is in a professional role with a person and (1) at the same time is in another role with the same person.... A psychologist refrains from entering into a multiple relationship if the multiple relationship could reasonably be expected to impair the psychologist's objectivity, competence, or effectiveness in performing his or her functions as a psychologist, or otherwise risks exploitation or harm to the person with whom the professional relationship exists.

Ethical Standard 3.04, Avoiding Harm

Psychologists take reasonable steps to avoid harming their clients/patients, students, supervisees, research participants, organizational clients, and others with whom they work, and to minimize harm where it is foreseeable and unavoidable.

In this case, the neuropsychologist transitioned from a clinical examiner to a treating doctor, back to an examiner, and then back to a treating doctor, all in the context of a medicolegal case. Such shifting of roles pits competing professional obligations against each other and in many contexts interferes with the provision of ethically appropriate services. Clinical examiners must maintain objectivity to the greatest extent possible so that personal feelings and therapeutic goals do not sway interpretations and opinions. In contrast, treating doctors often serve patients well by allying their goals with those of patients, wanting the best for them, and advocating for their needs and interests. These factors, which can be important for therapeutic alliance and treatment outcomes, naturally bias treating doctors in favor of their patients. Although an appropriate transition can be made from objective examiner to appropriately biased treating doctor, a neuropsychologist's ability to effectively transition from treating doctor to objective examiner will be limited by the preestablished therapeutic alliance. In addition, serving simultaneously as both treating doctor and clinical or forensic examiner represents a multiple relationship that could reasonably be expected to impair the examiner's objectivity and effectiveness.

In addition to having therapeutic alliances threaten the validity of evaluation results, the evaluation process and results may adversely affect treatment. A host of emotional reactions, such as feeling "stupid" or feeling that one is being judged critically, are more acceptable when elicited from a neutral examiner than from one's treating neuropsychologist, whose role tends to involve empowering the patient and providing empathic support. Patients who agree to be tested by their treating neuropsychologists are probably unaware of the potential risks associated with multiple relationships and therefore cannot make informed decisions about participation and referral options.

In certain settings, such as some medical or rehabilitation units or rural communities in which only one neuropsychologist is available to perform both serial evaluations and treatment, the benefit of having a conscientious clinician perform both services may outweigh the risks of harm or exploitation. However, in settings in which two or more qualified neuropsychologists practice, because of the unnecessary risk of harm clinicians should carefully consider the best interests of patients and their own motivations prior to conducting evaluations of patients they are treating.

In addition to mixing evaluation and treatment services, the neuropsychologist in this case, if not careful to maintain boundaries, is at risk of violating ethical standards of practice by combining clinical and forensic roles (Bush, 2005b; Bush, Connell, & Denney, 2006; Fisher, Johnson-Greene, & Barth, 2002; Iverson, 2000a; Sweet, Grote, & van Gorp, 2002). Bush (2005b) distinguished between the roles of forensic examiner, clinical examiner, and treating doctor. Forensic examiners and clinical examiners must maintain objectivity in all aspects of the examination process and critically assess the information and data obtained, whereas a treating doctor is typically accepting of the patient's reported experiences, is invested in the patient's well-being, and may at times advocate for the patient. Forensic evaluations should not be performed by treating doctors because the objectivity required for critical review of data and evaluation of alternative hypotheses is reduced to unacceptable levels. Thus, serving as both treating doctor and forensic expert represents a conflict of interest (Ethical Standard 3.06) and an inappropriate multiple relationship.

Although not (yet) requested of the neuropsychologist in this case, treating doctors that perform forensic examinations of their patients or write forensic reports have entered multiple relationships with conflicting interests that impair their objectivity and have a high likelihood of being harmful to the parties involved. If you proclaim in a report that you have considered and attempted to limit potential biases, you will signal the examiner's awareness of threats to objectivity, and you do not make the statement true. Instead such statements, when provided by treating doctors, reflect an awareness of the ethical issues and an intentional dismissal of the appropriate option of referring the patient to a colleague to perform the forensic service.

CASE 5.2

A neuropsychologist is contacted by a director of special education regarding an 11-year-old student who has recently experienced a decline in his behavior and academic performance at school and would benefit from a neuropsychological evaluation at the school district's expense. The child's mother states that the school has been unsuccessful in addressing her son's behavior and learning needs. The neuropsychologist obtains informed consent from the mother to perform the evaluation and provide copies of the report to both the mother and the school district. The neuropsychologist performs the evaluation and determines that problems in the home are largely responsible for the child's recent behavioral and academic problems. When these findings are conveyed sensitively to the child's mother, she becomes angry, accuses the neuropsychologist of colluding with the school, and states that the neuropsychologist must not release the report or findings to school officials or she will file a complaint with the state board of psychology. The neuropsychologist states that the report was already sent.

■ ■ ■

Ethical Standard 3.07, Third-Party Requests for Services

When psychologists agree to provide services to a person or entity at the request of a third party, psychologists attempt to clarify at the outset of the service the nature of the relationship with all individuals or organizations involved. This clarification includes the role of the psychologist (e.g., therapist, consultant, diagnostician, or expert witness), an identification of who is the client, the probable uses of the services provided or the information obtained, and the fact that there may be limits to confidentiality.

The neuropsychologist in this case appropriately clarified, verbally and in writing, with all parties at the outset of the relationships with the school district and the child's mother the manner in which the evaluation results would be disseminated. Although the child's mother apparently rejected findings and recommendations that might help her son, the neuropsychologist's behavior was ethical, and a complaint to the state board for psychology would likely be dismissed after a brief investigation.

CASE 5.3

A new adult patient is seen for an initial clinical interview. She reports that she recently underwent a neuropsychological evaluation and began treatment with a clinician across town but did not want to continue with him because she did not like his abrasive interpersonal style. The second neuropsychologist was very familiar with the prior clinician through opposing forensic activities, and long-standing animosity existed between them. The patient stated that she would have the prior neuropsychologist send her test report and other records to the second neuropsychologist. After multiple verbal and written requests for the records by both the patient and the new neuropsychologist over the course of six weeks, the second neuropsychologist sent a certified letter to the first neuropsychologist stating that if the records were not received within two weeks, a complaint would be filed with the state board for psychology.

Ethical Standard 3.09, Cooperation With Other Professionals

When indicated and professionally appropriate, psychologists cooperate with other professionals in order to serve their clients/patients effectively and appropriately.

By failing to provide appropriately requested records to a colleague as well as to the patient as required by law, the first neuropsychologist violated Ethical Standard 3.09 and obstructed the patient's subsequent neuropsychological treatment, potentially harming the patient. The first neuropsychologist let personal feelings toward a colleague and a possible narcissistic injury affect professional decisions and behavior, to the detriment of the patient. The second neuropsychologist's actions were appropriate.

CASE 5.4

A hospital-based, English-speaking neuropsychologist is referred a patient who is primarily Hungarian-speaking and who sustained a severe traumatic brain injury at work. The neuropsychologist decides that the patient, when accompanied by his wife who speaks slightly more English, is able to sufficiently understand the purpose, nature, and potential risks associated with the evaluation. As a result, the neuropsychologist has the patient sign the consent form, and the evaluation, emphasizing nonverbal tests and a cautious approach to interpretation, is performed with the patient's wife present to help with communication.

■ ■ ■

Ethical Standard 3.10, Informed Consent

(a) When psychologists conduct research or provide assessment, therapy, counseling, or consulting services in person or via electronic transmission or other forms of communication, they obtain the informed consent of the individual or individuals using language that is reasonably understandable to that person or persons except when conducting such activities without consent is mandated by law or governmental regulation or as otherwise provided in this Ethics Code.

(b) For persons who are legally incapable of giving informed consent, psychologists nevertheless (1) provide an appropriate explanation, (2) seek the individual's assent, (3) consider such persons' preferences and best interests, and (4) obtain appropriate permission from a legally authorized person, if such substitute consent is permitted or required by law. When consent by a legally authorized person is not permitted or required by law, psychologists take reasonable steps to protect the individual's rights and welfare.

(c) When psychological services are court ordered or otherwise mandated, psychologists inform the individual of the nature of the anticipated services, including whether the services are court ordered or mandated and any limits of confidentiality, before proceeding.

(d) Psychologists appropriately document written or oral consent, permission, and assent.

Case 5.4 consists of multiple ethical problems, including mishandling of the critically important informed consent process (Ethical Standards 3.10 and 9.03). As stated by Johnson-Greene and colleagues (Johnson-Green & the NAN Policy & Planning Committee, 2005), "Informed consent is decidedly the starting point for the patient-provider relationship and the genesis of the three key elements of ethical behavior: autonomy, nonmaleficence, and beneficence."[1]

---

[1] Sample informed consent forms are available online from the National Academy of Neuropsychology (www.nanonline.org) as appendixes to the position papers by Bush et al. (2005b) and Johnson-Greene and NAN Policy and Planning Committee (2005).

Ideally, with competent adults or patients' legal representatives, informed consent is a collaborative process of shared decision making in which mutually agreed-on goals are identified and the manner in which the goals with be pursued is specified (Knapp & VandeCreek, 2006). Knapp and VandeCreek (2006) described the differences between the medicolegal model of informed consent that has traditionally been used in medicine and the participatory model of informed consent that tends to be more appropriate for psychotherapy (see table 5.1). For situations in which the evaluation is likely the only neuropsychological services that will be provided, the medicolegal model may be most appropriate. In contrast, when ongoing neuropsychological treatment or combined evaluation and treatment are anticipated, the participatory model would be indicated. Neuropsychologists should consider whether one or both models of informed consent is best for their specific practices.

The neuropsychologist in case 5.4 cannot be confident that the patient fully understood the information that was conveyed, because of his very limited understanding of English, even with his wife's assistance, and his severe traumatic brain injury. It is more likely that the patient did not understand the information and was therefore not in a position to provide informed consent. The neuropsychologist apparently did not attempt to obtain the services of an appropriate interpreter or determine if a Hungarian-speaking colleague could be located. The results of the evaluation will be

Table 5.1 A Comparison of Medicolegal and Participatory Models of Informed Consent

MEDICOLEGAL MODEL	PARTICIPATORY MODEL
A passive activity	An interactive activity
A specific event	A fluid process
Dichotomous process (fixed treatment option)	Continuous process (multiple options)
Dichotomous outcome (accept/reject)	Consent exists on a continuum
Ability to consent is a fixed trait	Ability to consent may vary

Source: Based on information from Knapp and VandeCreek (2006).

virtually meaningless and, depending on the use to which they are put, will have a high likelihood of being harmful to the patient.

When determining whether to perform neuropsychological testing with examinees who have limited English language skills or are not representative of the dominant culture, clinicians must carefully weigh the potential benefits against the possible risks; the harm that can occur from an inappropriate evaluation of patients from diverse backgrounds is significant (Artiola i Fortuny & Mullaney, 1998; Brickman, Cabo, & Manly, 2006; Dede, 2005; Iverson, 2000b; Iverson, & Slick, 2003; Manly & Jacobs, 2002; Martin, 2005). Similarly, when considering evaluating or treating patients with compromised neurocognitive functioning, special care must be taken to maximize their rights and autonomy. "The freedom of competent adults to allow or restrict access to their bodies, thoughts, and feelings has long been a fundamental value of medicine and the cornerstone of clinical psychology, and neuropsychologists are obligated to defend that value" (Bush & Martin, forthcoming).

Learning Exercises

1. Describe possible multiple relationships that may emerge in your practice setting. How can you avoid potentially harmful multiple relationships in your practice?

2. Describe an ethical challenge that you have encountered or may anticipate based on your interaction or collaboration with other neuropsychologists. How did or would you resolve it?

3. Describe an ethical challenge that you have encountered or anticipate based on your interaction or collaboration with professionals from other disciplines. How did or would you resolve it?

4. How would you handle the informed consent process for persons who are legally incapable of giving informed consent?

6

██ ██ ██

Privacy and Confidentiality

The ability of patients to communicate openly and honestly has traditionally been a fundamental component of psychological treatment. In psychotherapy, patients must be confident that their most sensitive and deeply held thoughts and feelings can be safely divulged. However, patient willingness to disclose information that could become a source of embarrassment or result in other harmful consequences is as important for neuropsychological evaluations as it is for treatment. The ability of neuropsychologists to obtain accurate and complete patient information is essential for diagnostic accuracy and clinical decision making.

Privacy, *confidentiality*, and *privilege* are related terms pertaining to the protection of communications from patients in professional contexts. Webster's 9th New Collegiate Dictionary (Merriam-Webster, 1988) defines *privacy* as "freedom from unauthorized intrusion" (p. 936). Privacy originates in the bioethical principle of respect for patient autonomy and reflects the right of individuals to self-determination regarding the uses of their thoughts, feelings, beliefs, and experiences.

Confidentiality indicates "intimacy or willingness to confide" (Merriam-Webster, 1988, p. 275). In terms of the disclosure of private information to the neuropsychologist, confidentiality is a subset of privacy. Confidentiality requires a professional relationship and represents the responsibility of the neuropsychologist to not disclose information shared by the patient in the professional relationship.

Privilege refers to "a right or immunity granted as a peculiar benefit, advantage, or favor" (Merriam-Webster, 1988, p. 936). Privilege relieves the neuropsychologist of the obligation to testify in court about a patient's communications; thus, it is a narrower concept than confidentiality. By invoking privilege, the patient prevents the neuropsychologist from testifying or releasing records about his or her intimate personal details (Behnke, Perlin, & Bernstein, 2003). By waiving privilege, the patient allows the neuropsychologist to testify or release records in a legal proceeding. Thus, privilege belongs to and is invoked or waived at the direction of the patient. Without a privilege statute or a common-law rule, a neuropsychologist can be charged with contempt of court for refusing to testify about information shared by a patient in a professional context (Smith-Bell & Winslade, 1999).

The ethical importance of privacy and confidentiality is reflected in the American Psychological Association (APA) Ethics Code (Ethical Standard 4). In addition, specific legal rights and restrictions regarding privacy have been established at both the federal and state levels. Although the word *privacy* is not specifically mentioned the U.S. Constitution, the U.S. Supreme Court has recognized privacy as a constitutional right (*Eisenstadt v. Baird*, 1972). However, the courts have also held that the value of human safety, especially for vulnerable individuals such as children and the elderly, outweighs the importance placed on a patient's right to privacy (*Tarasoff v. Regents of the University of California*, 1976).

The HIPAA privacy rule is the aspect of the Health Insurance Portability and Accountability Act that addresses the privacy of health care information. Section 160.102(3) states that the privacy rule applies to practitioners who transmit protected health information in electronic form (including fax); however, the rule applies to all of a covered practitioner's health-related information, not just what is transmitted electronically (Behnke, Perlin, & Bernstein, 2003).

Rights to privacy and confidentiality differ between clinical and forensic contexts. When an individual places his or her mental state at issue in a legal matter, certain rights are waived in the interest of justice, including the right to privacy of relevant information. Discovery requirements allow the defense (in civil litigation) access to all relevant information, including neuropsychological records. Additionally, HIPAA constraints are limited in forensic evaluation contexts (Connell & Koocher, 2003; Fisher, 2003). For example, HIPAA's privacy rule allows covered practitioners to disclose protected health information in response to a court order (§164.524).

Despite the traditional emphasis on confidentiality in psychological treatment, most neuropsychological evaluations are performed with the advanced knowledge and expectation of all parties that the results will be shared with others, such as a referring doctor, an attorney, a family member, a school district, or another party with an appropriate interest in the results. With the exception of examinees with severe neurocognitive impairment, individuals referred for neuropsychological evaluations typically understand before they first establish contact with the neuropsychologist that the information they provide and the results of the evaluation will be shared with others. Nevertheless, because patients may not be fully aware of the limits to confidentiality, neuropsychologists have a fundamental responsibility to describe to all relevant parties the foreseeable limits to confidentiality and the anticipated uses of the information obtained and findings generated.

With some exceptions, examinees have the right to rescind their previously provided consent to have personal information, including neuropsychological test results, released to third parties. Rescinding consent, however, is equivalent to breaking a promise and places the neuropsychologist in an awkward position with regard to the referral source, payor, and other involved parties after performing an evaluation in good faith.

Multiple threats to confidentiality exist for clinical neuropsychologists and their patients. Examples of these threats in neuropsychological practice include the following (Bush & Martin, forthcoming): (1) practical limitations associated with inpatient settings, such as roommates; (2) a team approach to evaluation and treatment; (3) third-party observers, such as interpreters and parents; (4) mandated reporting requirements, such as an intent to harm oneself or others; (5) government monitoring of services funded by public payers such as Medicare; (6) managed care oversight, including utilization review; (7) practitioner disclosure to resolve unpaid debts; (8) electronic storage and transfer of patient information; (9) litigation; and (10) requests for services by third parties, such as employers and disability insurance carriers. The examples listed here do not include a client's request for the practitioner to disclose information or a patient's waiver of privilege in litigated matters.

CASE 6.1

A neuropsychologist conducts a brief bedside evaluation in a skilled nursing facility. During the evaluation, a nurse brings the patient's roommate back to the room for a respiratory treatment. Later, cleaned laundry is returned to the room, and the woman delivering the laundry leaves the door open on her way out. The patient says that he does not mind the intrusions and has nothing to hide. The evaluation is completed; at the nurse's station, the neuropsychologist informs the attending physician of the findings. The neuropsychologist then enters the test scores and a summary of the findings into the electronic medical record.

Ethical Standard 4.01, Maintaining Confidentiality

Psychologists have a primary obligation and take reasonable precautions to protect confidential information obtained through or stored in any medium, recognizing that the extent and limits of confidentiality may be regulated by law or established by institutional rules or professional or scientific relationship.

Case 6.1 reflects multiple threats to the patient's privacy and confidentiality. Although many practice contexts are fraught with possible intrusions on the evaluation process that cannot be completely avoided, it is often possible to take steps to minimize the potential for others to overhear or otherwise discover information conveyed by or about patients. For example, in this case, prior to beginning the evaluation the neuropsychologist could have asked the nurse if any treatments were planned for the patient or his roommate, or if there would be any other reason to expect a nurse or aid to enter the room. The neuropsychologist might also have asked the nurse or the patient's aid to help maintain privacy in the event that other staff, residents, or family were observed approaching the room. Finally, the neuropsychologist could have posted a "do not disturb" sign on the door to the patient's room.

In addition to the evaluation context, the discussion of the results at the nurse's station posed a potential threat to the patient's privacy. Such areas are often busy, with other staff, family members, and residents coming, going, and loitering. Neuropsychologists should attempt to maximize patient privacy when reporting evaluation results.

Ethical Decision Making in Clinical Neuropsychology

Ethical Standard 4.02, Discussing the Limits of Confidentiality

(a) Psychologists discuss with persons (including, to the extent feasible, persons who are legally incapable of giving informed consent and their legal representatives) and organizations with whom they establish a scientific or professional relationship (1) the relevant limits of confidentiality and (2) the foreseeable uses of the information generated through their psychological activities.

(b) Unless it is not feasible or is contraindicated, the discussion of confidentiality occurs at the outset of the relationship and thereafter as new circumstances may warrant.

(c) Psychologists who offer services, products, or information via electronic transmission inform clients/patients of the risks to privacy and limits of confidentiality.

The extent to which the neuropsychologist in case 6.1 discussed the limits of confidentiality with the patient is unknown. However, it is unlikely that the neuropsychologist could have predicted that the patient's roommate, the nurse, the woman delivering laundry, people near the nurse's station, and unknown others with access to the electronic medical record would come to learn about the patient's personal history and neurocognitive and emotional functioning. However, the neuropsychologist probably could have predicted that the patient's privacy in that setting could not be assured and should have given him the opportunity to decline the evaluation.

CASE 6.2

An 18-year-old undergoes a neuropsychological evaluation to clarify learning problems that emerged during his first semester of college. The neuropsychologist conducts a thorough interview and finds that in addition to problems keeping up with the pace of college lectures and difficulty structuring study time, the examinee is experiencing conflicting feelings about his sexuality. The examinee states that he has just recently acknowledged to himself that he is gay, and he has never before told anyone about these feelings. The neuropsychologist completes the evaluation and finds that the examinee has a verbal learning disorder for which he compensated well in high school but cannot overcome at the college level without accommodations. Psychological factors are not considered to be affecting neurocognitive functioning. In his report, the neuropsychologist provides not only the neurocognitive findings but also a comprehensive review of the examinee's background information, including a description of his recently discovered homosexuality.

■ ■ ■

Ethical Standard 4.04, Minimizing Intrusions on Privacy

(a) Psychologists include in written and oral reports and consultations, only information germane to the purpose for which the communication is made.

Ethical Standard 4.05, Disclosures

(a) Psychologists may disclose confidential information with the appropriate consent of the organizational client, the individual client/patient, or another legally authorized person on behalf of the client/patient unless prohibited by law.

(b) Psychologists disclose confidential information without the consent of the individual only as mandated by law, or where permitted by law for a valid purpose such as to (1) provide needed professional services; (2) obtain appropriate professional consultations; (3) protect the client/patient, psychologist, or others from harm; or (4) obtain payment for services from a client/patient, in which instance disclosure is limited to the minimum that is necessary to achieve the purpose.

The neuropsychologist in this case revealed very sensitive personal information about the examinee that was not germane for the purposes of the evaluation. The information about the examinee's sexuality added nothing to the understanding of his learning problems and was included in the report without the examinee's knowledge or approval. Beauchamp and Childress (2001) stated, "We necessarily surrender some of our privacy when we grant others access to our personal histories and bodies, but we also retain some control over information generated about us, at least in diagnostic and therapeutic contexts and in research" (p. 303). However, because of the actions of this neuropsychologist, the examinee did not have the control over his personal information to which he was entitled. To guard against harm from unauthorized disclosures, neuropsychologists will be well served by limiting information in reports to what has direct relevance on the referral question and seeking clarification from examinees when in doubt about whether to include sensitive information.

Learning Exercises

1. Describe at least three threats to confidentiality in your practice setting(s) and the ways in which you overcome such threats.

2. Describe the differences between privacy, confidentiality, and privilege.

3. List five examples of threats to confidentiality in neuropsychological practice.

7

■ ■ ■

Advertising and Other Public Statements

Many opportunities exist for neuropsychologists to educate consumers and recipients of services, referral sources, colleagues, the public, and others about neuropsychology in general and their services in particular. In addition, neuropsychological evaluation results and treatment status are conveyed to patients, referral sources, courts, and other relevant parties. The provision of complete and accurate information, privately or publicly, is consistent with the ethical principles of beneficence, nonmaleficence, integrity, and to the extent that such information is used to make decisions about the use of neuropsychological services, respect for autonomy.

In most practice settings, neuropsychological services are used to generate income for oneself or for one's employer, so there is often a competitive component to neuropsychological practice. Such competition provides incentive to make one's practice appear preferable to that of colleagues, potentially leading to exaggeration of credentials or experience or unsupportable statements of superiority. Gaudy advertisements, although possibly appearing unprofessional or distasteful, are not unethical. However, providing information that is inaccurate, incomplete, or may be otherwise misleading is inconsistent with ethical conduct.

CASE 7.1

A neuropsychologist in independent practice hires a consultant to develop a Web site for his practice. His site describes him as a specialist in numerous psychological specialties and aspects of practice and lists his credentials, including his doctorate, licensure, memberships in professional organizations, and board eligibility. In addition, his Web site states that he has lectured internationally (he does not reveal that he based that statement on his presentation of one poster at an conference in the United States) and is a faculty member of a local prestigious medical school (based on having once supervised a neuropsychology intern there). His site further indicates that he has testified more than 300 times, and it provides a testimonial from an attorney stating the neuropsychologist is well respected as an expert witness.

Ethical Standard 5.01, Avoidance of False or Deceptive Statements

(a) Public statements include but are not limited to paid or unpaid advertising, product endorsements, grant applications, licensing applications, other credentialing applications, brochures, printed matter, directory listings, personal resumes or curricula vitae, or comments for use in media such as print or electronic transmission, statements in legal proceedings, lectures and public oral presentations, and published materials. Psychologists do not knowingly make public statements that are false, deceptive, or fraudulent concerning their research, practice, or other work activities or those of persons or organizations with which they are affiliated.

This neuropsychologist engaged in both puffery and deception, some of which may have been unintentional. He exaggerated at least a few of his accomplishments and credentials. Using designations or terms that are understood by members of the profession but can be misleading to the public (e.g., ABD, doctoral candidate, board eligible) should be avoided. Only obtained credentials should be used, and terms such as *ABD*, *doctoral candidate*, and *board eligible* are not credentials. Similarly, vanity credentials—those that are awarded without a legitimate examination or peer review process—are deceptive and potentially harmful and should be avoided.

When describing products or services, particularly those that are novel or part of an emerging area of practice (e.g., Internet-based testing), it may be tempting to make statements that exceed the established scientific basis of the product or service. Because of the high likelihood of misleading the public or other unsophisticated consumers and thus impeding their ability to make informed decisions, it is important to avoid sensationalistic statements about one's products or services. Neuropsychologists who retain others for marketing and publicity purposes are responsible for the statements made and advertisements generated by such parties (Ethical Standard 5.02, Statements by Others).

CASE 7.2

A neuropsychologist takes the stand in a medical malpractice case to provide testimony regarding an examinee who experienced a brief period of anoxia associated with complications of a coronary artery bypass graft. She begins by accurately describing her credentials and experience. She then presents the results of her evaluation and her opinion that the examinee has a severe and permanent neurocognitive disability as a result of the problems encountered during surgery. She states that the results of her thorough assessment of symptom validity, which consisted of what she describes as the very sensitive Rey 15-Item Memory Test, preclude the possibility of malingering. She concludes by stating that neuropsychological research has established that anoxia for any amount of time usually causes severe and permanent brain damage.

Ethical Standard 5.01, Avoidance of False or Deceptive Statements

(b) Psychologists do not make false, deceptive, or fraudulent statements concerning (1) their training, experience, or competence;

(2) their academic degrees; (3) their credentials; (4) their institutional or association affiliations; (5) their services; (6) the scientific or clinical basis for, or results or degree of success of, their services; (7) their fees; or (8) their publications or research findings.

The neuropsychologist in this case clearly made statements that were inaccurate and misleading. Because she made the statements under oath, there are legal as well as ethical implications. However, it may be difficult to determine whether she intentionally provided false and deceptive statements or is just an incompetent practitioner presenting the information as she understands it. Depending on the sophistication of the defense attorney and the opportunity afforded to the defense's neuropsychology expert, the opportunity exists for the trier of fact to have the inaccurate information correct. Nevertheless, it may be difficult for a jury to understand the nuances of symptom validity assessment or to know which expert is right about the likely effects of an acquired brain injury. Omission of important information can be just as misleading and potentially harmful as false or deceptive statements.

Neuropsychologists providing testimony should regularly review their methods and statements in the context of ethical decision making. According to Johnson-Greene (in Bush et al., 2007), "As neuropsychologists we need to be knowledgeable about both ethical content as well as the process of ethical decision-making to function at an advanced level of practice." In the same article, Grote noted, "Of course, neither process nor content are of any use in the area of ethics if a supportive framework of personal integrity and a desire to "do good" for others is not in place. On a related matter, Johnson-Greene also stated, "I think if you follow the money you begin to understand why some of our neuropsychology colleagues who are otherwise reasonable and conscientious people have occasionally set aside their ethical standards."

The importance of the personal integrity of neuropsychologists for the welfare of consumers and the professional cannot be overemphasized. As Koocher and Keith-Spiegel (1998) stated, "The degree to which the public can trust a profession is ultimately determined by its members' collective commitment to integrity" (p. 27).

Learning Exercise

1. Describe an appropriate Web site for a neuropsychological practice. List the content that you consider to be (a) essential to include; (b) acceptable but not necessary to include; and (c) inappropriate to include. When considering links to other sites, keep in mind that the information found on other Web sites may be outdated or otherwise inaccurate and adversely affect those who use the information.

8

■■■

Record Keeping and Fees

This chapter addresses the ethical issues associated with the creation and management of records and financial practices. Because of their unique issues, record keeping and financial matters are addressed separately.

Record Keeping

Appropriate record keeping benefits neuropsychologists and clients. Accurate and complete documentation of neuropsychological services serves several purposes. Such documentation (1) communicates neuropsychological evaluation results or neuropsychological status as evident during treatment; (2) facilitates the provision of ongoing treatment by describing treatment plans, services provided, and patient progress; (3) facilitates the provision of subsequent services by the same clinician or another practitioner at a later time; and (4) allows reviewers to determine whether the services provided were appropriate and opinions generated were valid. In addition, appropriate documentation is typically required for third-party reimbursement. For these reasons, accurate and complete documentation of neuropsychological services is essential for ethical and legal practice. For a reviewer to determine accuracy and completeness, records must be clearly identified as the product of the treating or examining neuropsychologist and must be legible.

CASE 8.1

A neuropsychologist performs a substantial amount of medicolegal work—that is, he provides clinical evaluations and ongoing treatment with patients who are involved in litigation following motor vehicle accidents. His initial consultation notes, which are often addressed to no-fault claims representatives, are typed on letterhead, as are his neuropsychological reports; however, the notes of his treatment sessions are handwritten, do not include any identifying information for him or the patients, and are largely illegible.

■ ■ ■

Ethical Standard 6.01, Documentation of Professional and Scientific Work and Maintenance of Records

Psychologists create, and to the extent the records are under their control, maintain, disseminate, store, retain, and dispose of records and data relating to their professional and scientific work in order to (1) facilitate provision of services later by them or by other professionals, (2) allow for replication of research design and analyses, (3) meet institutional requirements, (4) ensure accuracy of billing and payments, and (5) ensure compliance with law.

The neuropsychologist in this case generates appropriate reports for the initial consultation and neuropsychological evaluation; however, his treatment notes lack essential identifying information as well as the clarity needed for readers to determine the nature and appropriateness of the treatment provided and the status of the patient. Such inappropriate documentation impedes the provision of clinical or forensic services by others. In this case, it is also peculiar that some reports are written to no-fault claims representative rather than referring doctors, a practice that raises questions about the clinical nature of the case.

Neuropsychologists and consumers of neuropsychological services typically expect that evaluation results will be appropriately documented and provided to the patient, referral source, or others. This expectation of releasing records contrasts with expectations in many psychotherapeutic contexts that documentation will be relatively limited and is not created for the purpose of dissemination. Additionally, neuropsychologists who provide forensic evaluation or other medicolegal services do so with the knowledge that their records will be critically reviewed by others, including colleagues.

"Documentation that is linked to a competent evaluation and is of sufficient detail to allow an independent peer reviewer to arrive at similar conclusions or clearly identify how the conclusions in a report or testimony were reached would most likely withstand adjudicative scrutiny" (Bush, Connell, & Denney, 2006, p. 92). State licensing laws and regulations typically establish minimum record-keeping requirements. Additionally, the American Psychological Association has provided *Record Keeping Guidelines* (APA, 1993) that "provide the ethical floor for psychologists but give little direction on the content of the records" (Knapp & VandeCreek, 2006, p. 125). At the time of this writing, a revision of the Record Keeping Guidelines (APA, 2006) is nearing completion and appears likely to provide additional guidance.

Jurisdictional laws typically govern access to records. According to the HIPAA Privacy Rule, patients have a right to access all the information in their medical records, except psychotherapy notes. Psychotherapy notes include documentation or analysis of conversations that occur during psychotherapy or counseling; they do not include session start and stop times, modalities and frequencies of treatment, or test results, nor do they include summaries of the diagnosis, functional status, treatment plan, symptoms, prognosis, or progress to date. State laws that grant greater patient access to their records take precedent over HIPAA's Privacy Rule.

Exceptions to the patient's right to access records exist when disclosure of the records would threaten the life or physical safety of the patient or a third party and in forensic contexts. In a clause relevant for forensic neuropsychology, HIPAA states that information compiled in anticipation of use in civil, criminal, and administrative proceedings is *not* subject to the same right of review and amendment as is health care information in general [§164.524(a)(1)(ii)] (U.S. Department of Health and Human Services, 2003). Nevertheless, because information compiled in forensic cases is disseminated to all invested parties, patients and other examinees will likely have ready access to the information if they so desire.

With of the increased focus on patient autonomy and the legal mandates that support the patient's right to autonomy, documentation should be prepared accordingly. Neuropsychologists should write reports and maintain records with the expectation that in addition to the referral source, patients, their families, the courts, or others may obtain access to the records. For this reason, neuropsychologists may be well served by using discretion in their choice of content for their records.

Some neuropsychologists, wishing to protect patient privacy or interfere with the professional activities of a colleague, may attempt to thwart disclosure of their records. Strategies used to prevent disclosure include (1) keeping minimal records, (2) keeping double sets of records, (3) coding information in their records, (4) doctoring or disposing of records or documents, or (5) outright lying (Barsky & Gould, 2002). Additional strategies include omitting information that identifies the clinician or the patient and writing illegible notes. These activities are inconsistent with ethical practice.

Neuropsychologists who provide services in organizations may face unique documentation requirements, in addition to those established by jurisdictional law. In particular, the use of electronic medical records raises questions about access to records and handling raw test data. As a result, the control, maintenance, and dissemination of records in organizational settings may pose unique ethical challenges. In such cases, neuropsychologists should make known their commitment to professional ethics and strive to maximize the security of patient information and test data, working with the organization's management as needed to ensure that appropriate safeguards exist.

Neuropsychologists who provide forensic services obtain considerable amounts of records from attorneys and other sources, and they generate their own records. From the moment that neuropsychologists know or reasonably should know that their data and the opinions derived therefrom will be used in litigation, they have a responsibility to create documentation with sufficient detail and quality to allow reasonable scrutiny by others (Committee on the Revision of the Ethical Guidelines for Forensic Psychologists, 2005). "This level of documentation ordinarily exceeds the level of documentation typically employed during the course of providing non-forensic evaluation and therapeutic services" (Committee on the Revision of the Ethical Guidelines for Forensic Psychologists, 2005, p. 27).

Although APA guidelines, state licensing board regulations, and state laws specify the length of time that records must be maintained in clinical cases, ambiguity exists in most jurisdictions regarding the length of time that records should be maintained in forensic cases. Often requirements pertain to psychological services in general, with no distinction made between clinical and forensic services. Based on information obtained from colleagues, unless otherwise specified by the jurisdictional law, the following general approach seems common. First, maintain all records obtained from other sources and generated by oneself until the completion of the case. Second, after the case has been concluded, maintain all records generated by oneself in a manner that is consistent with jurisdictional laws or APA guidelines, complying with whichever requirement specifies the longer period of time, and appropriately dispose of records obtain from other sources if desired. Third, after the time specified by jurisdictional law and APA has passed, maintain copies of evaluation reports and potentially important notes as desired, in an electronic format if preferred, and appropriately dispose of all other records. Fourth, ensure that preparations have been made for the appropriate transfer or disposal of records following retirement or death. Of note, the statute of limitations on malpractice suits in the United States, though varying between states, is typically 2 years for adults and 2 years after minors turn 18 (Knapp & VandeCreek, 2006).

Billing Issues

Billing and other financial matters vary considerably depending on the nature of one's practice. The primary commonality is that arrangements must be specified and agreed on, preferably in writing, by all parties in advance. In addition, contingencies for nonpayment should be included when establishing and discussing fees. Three issues are addressed in this section: referral fees, contingency fees, and withholding reports until fees are paid.

Referral fees are payments made by a practitioner to another professional for referring a patient for services. Sometimes described as "fee splitting," this arrangement is inappropriate because paying for referrals has the potential to result in improper referrals. In contrast, fees can ethically be divided between professionals if they are based on the service provided rather than on the referral itself (Ethical Standard 6.07, Referrals and Fees). For example, neuropsychologists can divide fees with other professionals in the context of employer–employee relationships, professional consultation, administrative support, or office rent.

Contingency fees are those fees that are contingent on the outcome litigation. Considerable potential for examiner bias exists when the nature of one's opinions have the potential to affect one's ability to get paid. For example, when retained by a plaintiff's attorney or providing clinical services in the context of litigation, statements that emphasize severity of impairment and disability and a causal relationship between the accident and the alleged injuries will increase the likelihood of a favorable financial outcome for the attorney or patient, thereby increasing the likelihood or amount that one will be paid. Such financial arrangements typically take the form of liens against lawsuits. In contrast, other lien or contingency arrangements that do not link the nature of one's opinions with one's ability to be compensated for services may be appropriate.

Neuropsychologists who perform evaluations in clinical settings commonly complete the evaluations, write and send reports, and bill for services. However, in some situations neuropsychologists may expect that payment will not be made after the report has been provided. In such cases, unless the information is needed for the examinee's emergency medical care, practitioners may withhold reports or other records until payment has been received (Ethical Standard 6.03, Withholding Records for Nonpayment). Consumers should be informed of fees and should understand that they are ultimately responsible for payment of services rendered. Consumers should agree to the fee requirements in writing.

CASE 8.2

A neuropsychologist obtains authorization from a managed care company to perform a comprehensive neuropsychological evaluation as an out-of-network provider. The managed care company will not indicate the exact amount that will be paid, nor will it provide specifics about the patient's deductible. The neuropsychologist informs the patient that the evaluation has been authorized and performs the evaluation. He provides the patient and the referring physician with verbal feedback and a copy of the report, and he bills the insurance company. Three months go by without payment, so he contacts the insurance company. He is told that payment was issued to the patient four weeks prior. He attempts to contact the patient but consistently reaches her voicemail, so he leaves messages asking to have his call returned. Two weeks later he receives a check for $350. He is unable to determine from the insurance company or the patient why the payment was so low. He sends a certified letter to the patient stating that she is responsible for the $2,150 balance. He receives a letter from her stating that she never agreed to any such thing and that she would file an ethics violation and possibly harassment charges if he persisted in contacting her. He realizes that his fee agreement does not list specific fees. He does not know what to do.

▦ ▦ ▦

Ethical Standard 6.04, Fees and Financial Arrangements

(a) As early as is feasible in a professional or scientific relationship, psychologists and recipients of psychological services reach an agreement specifying compensation and billing arrangements.

Billing policies should be described at the outset of the professional relationship, and all relevant parties should understand and agree to the amount, method, and timing of payment, as well as to the steps taken if payment is not received. The potential for billing problems to reach significant levels can occur for neuropsychologists, compared with psychologists in other areas of practice, because large debts can accrue quickly. For example, a comprehensive evaluation that takes place in one day and goes unpaid may result in an immediate debt in the thousands of dollars. The neuropsychologist in this case failed to obtain the necessary agreement from the patient before performing the evaluation, thus risking not getting paid in full (if at all). He is left with a difficult decision about how to proceed. Although collection agencies can be used to collect unpaid fees, as Knapp and VandeCreek stated, "Occasionally writing off an unpaid bill may be more expedient in the long run than facing allegations of misconduct, even if they are frivolous" (2006, p. 153).

Learning Exercises

1. **Describe four purposes served by accurate and complete record keeping.**

2. **In addition to the Ethics Code, what APA publication provides information regarding appropriate creation and management of records?**

3. The length of time that records should be maintained in forensic cases is not well established. Describe the four-stage approach presented in this chapter.

4. Develop a fee arrangement to be used in a neuropsychological practice context different from yours.

9

■ ■ ■

Education, Training, Research, and Publication

The two academically focused sections of the Ethics Code (Ethical Standard 7, Education and Training, and Ethical Standard 8, Research and Publication) are discussed in this chapter. These sections are presented together because, although it is critically important to neuropsychological ethics, neuropsychologists spend relatively little professional time engaged in these activities compared with clinical activities. Sweet and colleagues (2002) found that about 9 percent of neuropsychologists' professional time per week is spent in teaching or training, and about 7 percent is spent conducting research, compared to about 70 percent spent in clinical activities. In addition, academically oriented activities result in relatively few ethics complaints and (in my experience) generate much less ethics discussion among clinical neuropsychologists than other professional activities. Thus, the briefer focus on ethical issues in academic activities occurs not because ethical dilemmas are less common, less changing, or less important in such activities but simply because clinical neuropsychologists as a group spend less time engaged in these activities than in applied activities.

Education and Training

As stated in chapter 4, professional competence is the foundation of ethical practice. Professional competence begins with education and training. As educators and supervisors, neuropsychologists have ethical obligations to advance the knowledge, skills, and personal development of their students; avoid harming their students; respect the autonomy of their students; treat their students fairly; and protect and enhance society by graduating or advancing only qualified individuals (Knapp & VandeCreek, 2006).

To fulfill ethical obligations, neuropsychologists must be competent in both the topics that they teach and teaching itself. The same mandate applies for supervision. Competent teachers and supervisors are not only knowledgeable and technically proficient but are also able to connect with others in a manner that allows them to best impart their knowledge and skills and promote the development of their students or supervisees. Neuropsychologists should continually examine their ability to achieve these goals and seek ways to improve, including eliciting feedback from students, supervisees, and colleagues.

Sensitivity to diversity is at least as important in teaching and training as it is in clinical activities. The importance of diversity in neuropsychology must be an essential aspect of all education and training programs. Neuropsychologists who teach or train others are not only imparting information, they are, knowingly or not, modeling behavior for future professionals. As a result, neuropsychologists must evaluate their own actions with an appreciation of how, through their positions of power, they influence students and supervisees and, by extension, affect the lives of those who will one day receive professional services from those students and supervisees.

CASE 9.1

A neuropsychologist is an adjunct member of the graduate faculty of a relatively new, nonaccredited neuropsychology doctoral program. The program director, with a knack for marketing, finds that chiropractors are very interested in the program and encourages their enrollment by advertising in chiropractic journals. As a result, the program has a high percentage of chiropractors as students. The chiropractors prove to be among the best students, highly motivated to learn neuropsychological testing and the business aspects of neuropsychological practice. After a few years, the neuropsychologist notices that most of the chiropractors leave the program after the third year and offer "neurocognitive mental examinations" in their offices, some through the use of technicians. She understands that the scope of practice law for chiropractors in her state allows them to evaluate mental state as part of their duties. The neuropsychologist is concerned that she is teaching and training other health care professionals to perform neuropsychological evaluations and that they are doing so without completing all of the necessary education and training, although they may be practicing within their scope of practice according to state law.

∎∎∎

Ethical Standard 7.01, Design of Education and Training Programs

Psychologists responsible for education and training programs take reasonable steps to ensure that the programs are designed to provide the appropriate knowledge and proper experiences, and to meet the requirements for licensure, certification, or other goals for which claims are made by the program.

The neuropsychologist in this case is concerned about her moral and ethical responsibilities to the public, the profession, and the academic program, including the students. With the exception of some chiropractors overstepping the boundaries of their competence by providing neuropsychological services without completing the educational and training requirements as established by professional organizations, the existence of ethical or legal violations is ambiguous. Clearly, aspirational ethical principles, such as beneficence and nonmaleficence, have been neglected, and a case could be made that ethical standards involving competence, bases for scientific and professional judgments, and avoiding harm and possibly some assessment standards are being violated; however, the activities of these health care professionals are subject to the laws and ethics that govern their profession. Practitioners of other health care specialties might consider three years in a neuropsychology doctoral program to be more than sufficient and may not appreciate the recommendations of National Academy of Neuropsychology and the APA Division of Neuropsychology, particularly if the practitioners of such professions are not using the word *neuropsychological* to describe their services.

Although it may not be appropriate to deny admission to qualified candidates on the basis of what they might do in the future, the neuropsychologist should discuss her concerns with the director of the program to determine if alternate marketing strategies should be pursued and if steps can be taken during the admissions process to better assess applicants' commitments to completing training. She may also have an obligation to pursue the matter informally with the individuals who are providing neuropsychological services without appropriate training, or pursue it formally through consultation with the regulatory bodies of their profession. Finally, she may want to reconsider her association with the program.

Research and Publication

When conducting research, neuropsychologists have a primary obligation to respect the autonomy of participants, safeguard their privacy, and protect them from harm, particularly when the research involves vulnerable populations. With few exceptions, participation in research should be voluntary, based on sufficient information for participants to make informed decisions about their participation, and free of deception. When the potential benefits of deception outweigh the risks and deception is deemed necessary, informed consent is usually obtained during the debriefing process, although debriefing at times may be withheld for scientific or humane reasons.

CASE 9.2

Dr. A is interested in advancing the ability of clinical neuropsychologists to determine adequate examinee effort from invalid effort. She develops a new symptom validity test that appears to assess working memory but really assesses effort. She informs the staff neuropsychologist that works for her to administer the test as part of the evaluations of all traumatic brain injury patients admitted to the unit in the next two weeks. She states that she has been doing so for the past two weeks and has obtained some very promising data.

Dr. A violated a number of ethical standards and has asked her junior colleague to do the same. Dr. A's standardization procedures are highly suspect (ES 9.05, Test Construction). She did not obtain approval from her facility's institutional review board (ES 8.01, Institutional Approval) and did not discuss the experimental nature of test with patients or their proxies and obtain their approval (ES 8.02, Informed Consent to Research). However, she may have believed that she was justified in forgoing the informed consent process (ES 8.05, Dispensing with Informed Consent for Research).

Ethical Standard 8.05, Dispensing With Informed Consent for Research

Psychologists may dispense with informed consent only (1) where research would not reasonably be assumed to create distress or harm and involves (a) the study of normal educational practices, curricula, or classroom management methods conducted in educational settings; (b) only anonymous questionnaires, naturalistic observations, or archival research for which disclosure of responses would not place participants at risk of criminal or civil liability or damage their financial standing, employability, or reputation, and confidentiality is protected; or (c) the study of factors related to job or organization effectiveness conducted in organizational settings for which there is no risk to participants' employability, and confidentiality is protected or (2) where otherwise permitted by law or federal or institutional regulations.

Including simple mental tasks that appeared to assess working memory in a more comprehensive neuropsychological evaluation likely posed very little risk of harm to the patients who were being used as research participants. Nevertheless, the patients were deceived.

Ethical Standard 8.07, Deception in Research

(a) Psychologists do not conduct a study involving deception unless they have determined that the use of deceptive techniques is justified by the study's significant prospective scientific, educational, or applied value and that effective nondeceptive alternative procedures are not feasible.

(b) Psychologists do not deceive prospective participants about research that is reasonably expected to cause physical pain or severe emotional distress.

(c) Psychologists explain any deception that is an integral feature of the design and conduct of an experiment to participants as early as is feasible, preferably at the conclusion of their participation, but no later than at the conclusion of the data collection, and permit participants to withdraw their data.

Symptom validity research often requires deception. Participants must believe that symptom validity tests are assessing memory or another neurocognitive construct other than effort. Thus, Dr. A may have been justified in not informing patients or their proxies of the nature of the study in advance. However, she should have debriefed the patients after obtaining the data (ES 8.08, Debriefing), and her failure to obtain review board approval of her study was significant. In addition, she attempted to use her position of influence to coerce a junior colleague to engage in similar ethical misconduct (ES 3.08, Exploitative Relationships). Whether Dr. A's dispensing with informed consent and her use of deception were appropriate may be matters for debate; however, such debate must occur with colleagues and the institutional review board prior to performing the research.

CASE 9.3

Dr. A and his colleagues are also interested in advancing the ability of clinical neuropsychologists to determine adequate examinee effort from invalid effort. They establish a known groups research design whereby performance on symptom validity indicators embedded within neurocognitive tests is compared across different clinical and forensic groups and an experimental group given instruction on how to feign neurocognitive impairment and avoid detection. These test coached participants are instructed how to feign cognitive impairment on neuropsychological tests and are taught test-taking strategies to help them avoid detection.

Determinations of examinee effort and honesty, needed to establish the validity of examinee's approach to the evaluation and test results, should be empirically based. Recent research on malingering involving a variety of methodologies has improved the ability of neuropsychologists to understand

and assess effort and honesty. One method involves coaching research participants to malinger. Because examinees, particularly in forensic contexts, are at times instructed by attorneys or others about symptom validity testing, it is important to understand how coached examinees perform on neuropsychological evaluations and symptom validity tests and indicators.

Coaching in the context of malingering research typically takes one of two forms: symptom coaching or test coaching (Powell, Gfeller, Hendricks, & Sharland, 2004). Such coaching has benefits and drawbacks. The benefits of test-coached malingering research include advancement of neuropsychological knowledge regarding symptom validity assessment, more accurate evaluation conclusions (GP A, Beneficence and Nonmaleficence), and fairer forensic determinations based on increased knowledge (GP D, Justice). In contrast, research participants taught to avoid detection of feigned neurocognitive impairment may later use the information to their own advantage in forensic contexts. Additionally, and potentially more problematic, participants may disseminate their new-found information on a large scale (e.g., via the Internet). Thus, test-coached malingering research places the security of symptom validity assessment methods in jeopardy.

Ethical Standard 9.11, Maintaining Test Security

The term test materials refers to manuals, instruments, protocols, and test questions or stimuli and does not include test data as defined in Standard 9.04, Release of Test Data. Psychologists make reasonable efforts to maintain the integrity and security of test materials and other assessment techniques consistent with law and contractual obligations, and in a manner that permits adherence to this Ethics Code.

Harmful outcomes of widespread dissemination of symptom validity assessment methods could include large-scale invalidation of future evaluation results, unfair legal determinations, and invalidated tests.

Given the potential benefits and potential harm of test coaching methodologies, deciding whether to instruct research participants how to beat these measures involves addressing an ethical dilemma. The selection of research methods requires careful consideration of the potential impact on both individuals and society. When choosing research methodology, researchers must weigh the relative importance of conflicting ethical principles and take reasonable steps to minimize harmful effects.

Learning Exercise

1. Approximately what percentage of professional time per week do clinical neuropsychologists spend in teaching or training?

   a. 9 percent

   b. 7 percent

   c. 70 percent

   d. To date, no surveys have been completed to address this question.

2. In addition to being competent in the subjects that they teach, neuropsychologists who teach should be competent in:

   a. core subjects in clinical psychology.

   b. teaching.

   c. research.

   d. information technology.

3. The use of deception in research may be justified by a study's significant prospective value in all of the following *except*:

   a. science.

   b. finance.

   c. education.

   d. clinical application.

10

■ ■ ■

Assessment

In terms of hours spent per week, assessment is by far the primary professional activity of clinical neuropsychologists (Sweet, Grote, & van Gorp, 2002). As a result, it seems reasonable to expect that neuropsychologists will most likely encounter ethical challenges in the context of assessment-related activities, either their own or those of colleagues. As Fisher and colleagues (2002) stated, "the very breadth and diversity that result in the richness of neuropsychological practice often leads to disagreements, conflicts, and uncertainties regarding optimal practice activities" (p. 3). In striving to avoid ethical misconduct and achieve high standards of ethical practice, neuropsychologists must familiarize themselves with the ethical challenges associated with test selection, use, and interpretation (Anderson & Palozzi, 2002; Fisher, Johnson-Greene, & Barth, 2002; McSweeny & Naugle, 2002; Thompson, 2002) and attempt to anticipate the unique aspects of such challenges in different practice contexts.

CASE 10.1

An 82-year-old man is brought for a neuropsychological evaluation by his son because of his concern that his father's increasing forgetfulness is a sign of Alzheimer's disease. He wonders if he should consider moving his father to an assisted living facility or at least have him eat more blueberries. The patient tells his son that he is no more forgetful than his friends, that he does need or want a neuropsychological evaluation, and that he will not take the evaluation seriously. Nevertheless, the patient's son drops him off at the neuropsychologist's office at the prearranged time. Following the informed consent presentation, the patient states that he will undergo the evaluation to pacify his son and signs the consent form. The neuropsychologist does not assess symptom validity quantitatively because he believes that "geriatric patients have no reason to malinger; they are more likely to minimize their problems and try their best so that they do not lose their independence," and he believes that he can tell when his patients are not trying their best. The clinical interview reveals hypertension and hypercholesterolemia, both controlled with medication, but the patient is otherwise healthy and able to live independently without problems. The test results reveal impaired performance in multiple cognitive domains but no clear pattern of deficits. The neuropsychologist believes that the data are most consistent with a multi-infarct process and recommends a supervised living arrangement.

Ethical Standard 9.01, Bases for Assessments

(a) Psychologists base the opinions contained in their recommendations, reports, and diagnostic or evaluative statements, including forensic testimony, on information and techniques sufficient to substantiate their findings.

(b) Except as noted in 9.01c, psychologists provide opinions of the psychological characteristics of individuals only after they have conducted an examination of the individuals adequate to support their statements or conclusions.

The neuropsychologist in this case made erroneous assumptions about both this geriatric patient's investment in the neuropsychological evaluation process and his own ability to subjectivity assess effort and symptom validity. Although it may be true that most geriatric patients respond honestly and try their best on neuropsychological tests and invalid responding likely occurs much less frequently with geriatric evaluations than forensic evaluations, the possibility exists that failing to assess symptom validity empirically will result in harmful conclusions for some percentage of patients.

Bush and colleagues (2005b) stated, "Although there is typically less incentive to mislead the examiner in clinical contexts than in forensic contexts, the potential for invalid performance due to intentional or unintentional exaggeration or fabrication remains . . . determinations regarding the validity of patient performance are generally aided by the inclusion of SVTs in neuropsychological evaluations" (p. 423). Additionally, Bush (forthcoming) stated, "Neuropsychologists are advised to be mindful of the ethical implications of symptom validity assessment, including its nonuse. In most settings, neuropsychological evaluations that do not include objective assessment of symptom validity with empirically derived measures and/or indicators are not consistent with ethical standards of practice."[1] In case 10.1, the patient's invalid performance occurred not because he wanted to feign impairment but because he did not consider the evaluation to be worth his effort.

In addition to not basing his opinions on sufficient assessment techniques, the neuropsychologist failed to interview the patient's son or obtain and review medical records. Furthermore, having arrived at the opinion that the patient was experiencing a multi-infarct dementia, the neuropsychologist also failed to refer the patient for additional medical examination, including neuroimaging, which would have helped clarify the diagnostic picture. Overall, the neuropsychologist did not have sufficient information to substantiate his diagnostic conclusions and recommendations, and the patient may suffer decreased autonomy and emotional distress as a result. It is unclear whether the neuropsychologist informed the patient during the consent process of the potential impact of the neuropsychological evaluation on his future independence (ES 9.03, Informed Consent in Assessments).

CASE 10.2

A 40-year-old woman with a master's degree in mechanical engineering is evaluated by a neuropsychologist because of prob-

---

[1] Iverson (2006) provides a comprehensive review of the ethical issues associated with symptom validity assessment in neuropsychology.

Assessment 85

lems with attention, memory, and executive functions four months after a ruptured anterior communicating artery aneurysm and neurosurgical clipping. The patient's husband reports that she is very distractible, impulsive, and irritable, and he is concerned about her ability to drive. The neuropsychologist performs a comprehensive evaluation. Based on normative data that were not corrected for age or education, the patient scores well above average in most neurocognitive domains, but she performs in the low average range with complex attention skills and executive functioning. Because none of her scores fell in the "impaired" range, the neuropsychologist concluded that her attention and executive functions, although low, were not sufficiently low to recommend that she discontinue driving.

Ethical Standard 9.06, Interpreting Assessment Results

When interpreting assessment results, including automated interpretations, psychologists take into account the purpose of the assessment as well as the various test factors, test-taking abilities, and other characteristics of the person being assessed, such as situational, personal, linguistic, and cultural differences, that might affect psychologists' judgments or reduce the accuracy of their interpretations. They indicate any significant limitations of their interpretations.

Because low average test performance for this patient may represent a significant decline from her preinjury abilities, the neuropsychologist apparently did not take into the patient's preinjury level of neurocognitive functioning when making determinations regarding impairment. In contrast, the neuropsychologist may be making his determinations based on the patient's absolute level of functioning. That is, compared to the general population, she performed no lower than the low average range, and a substantial percentage of the population functions normally, including driving, at that level of intellectual and neurocognitive ability. Although the use of appropriate age- and education-corrected norms would have resulted in the patient's complex attention and executive function scores being classified at some level of impairment, the relationship between the impaired scores and daily functioning is not well established (Sbordone & Long, 1996). The neuropsychologist may also have considered that the value of neuropsychological tests for predicting driving safety has not yet been established.

This case demonstrates a primary challenge to the interpretation of neuropsychological data in some cases: the availability, selection, and use of appropriate normative data. In addition, the performance ranges used to describe patients' test results vary among clinicians and sometimes by the same clinician. Finally, the case raises the challenges inherent in predicting from neuropsychological test results a patient's ability to independently and safely perform various functional activities. Ethical practice requires clinicians to attend to these practice issues, relying on neuropsychological science to the extent possible, acknowledging limitations and justifying decisions as needed, and carefully weighing issues of patient autonomy and safety, erring on the side of safety.

CASE 10.3

A neuropsychologist develops a brief, computer-based test to diagnose Alzheimer's disease. The test has excellent psychometric properties when used in the lab and draws the attention of a pharmaceutical company when the reliability and validity studies are presented at a conference. With funding from the pharmaceutical company, the neuropsychologist is able to make the test available on the Internet, with the goal of reaching people who otherwise might not seek or be able to receive neuropsychological services. She includes cautionary statements that emphasize the importance of confirming the results with appropriate health care providers. Unknown to her, a 68-year-old widowed woman with a seventh-grade education who is living alone in Poland takes the Polish translation of the test. She has noticed increased forgetfulness in recent years. During her monthly visit to her son's home, he sets her up at his computer to take the test and provides assistance as needed. She scores in the "moderate Alzheimer's" range.

After returning home, she becomes very depressed and with-drawn, and she does not show up at her son's home the following month.

Ethical Standard 9.09, Test Scoring and Interpretation Services

(c) Psychologists retain responsibility for the appropriate application, interpretation, and use of assessment instruments, whether they score and interpret such tests themselves or use automated or other services.

Ethical Standard 9.10, Explaining Assessment Results

Regardless of whether the scoring and interpretation are done by psychologists, by employees or assistants, or by automated or other outside services, psychologists take reasonable steps to ensure that explanations of results are given to the individual or designated representative unless the nature of the relationship precludes provision of an explanation of results (such as in some organizational consulting, preemployment or security screenings, and forensic evaluations), and this fact has been clearly explained to the person being assessed in advance.

Internet-based neuropsychological evaluation and diagnostic services pose unique ethical challenges or rare twists to old challenges. Despite the exponential increase in the ownership and use of computers in recent years, neuropsychologists have few published resources to guide the practice of neuropsychological assessment (Schatz, 2005). "In fact, the term 'Internet' appears only twice in the 200 Ethics Code, 'technology' only once, and 'electronic' five times. Rather, practicing psychologists are left to extrapolate proper ethical conduct to those areas where use of emergent technologies may affect the means by which they carry out their practice" (Schatz, 2005, p. 193).

The neuropsychologist in this case provided neurocognitive testing and diagnostic information to an unknown person and without having any control over the testing environment (Ethical Standards 9.01, Bases of Assessments; 9.02, Use of Assessments; 9.06, Interpreting Assessment Results; and

9.09, Test Scoring and Interpretation Services). With regard to computer-based assessment, Browndyke (2005) stated,

> When considering participant appropriateness or the validity of results derived from computerized assessment measures, idiosyncratic (e.g., lack of computer familiarity, computer-related anxiety), environmental (e.g., apparatus ergonomics, technological barriers), and measurement (e.g., measure's applicability in participant population) factors should be taken into account. (p. 185)

Internet-based evaluations are unable to account for these factors.

The neuropsychologist in this case was also unable to discuss the test results in the context the woman's life or to provide specific recommendations or follow through (ES 9.10, Explaining Assessment Results). In addition, the test, although translated to Polish, was not standardized on persons who are demographically similar to the woman taking the test (ES 9.05, Test Construction).

Test security was another issue of ethical concern in this case (ES 9.11, Maintaining Test Security). As Schatz (2005) stated, "Use of Internet technology creates an inherently paradoxical arrangement in which the mechanism for the viewing content (i.e., the web browser) may actually store the document in memory or in a cache file, or facilitate the creation of copies of source material by the user" (p. 196). Test security, essential for valid neuropsychological assessment, cannot be maintained with Internet-based administration. Sacrificing test integrity and security by using Internet-based administration can have devastating effects, the specifics of which are unknown to test developers and administrators.

The intersection of neuropsychology with information technology and telecommunications offers exciting possibilities, enticing neuropsychologists to pursue emerging technologies and the promise of improved and increased assessment possibilities (Bush, Naugle, & Johnson-Greene, 2002). New frontiers bring new responsibilities as well as possibilities. In all instances, neuropsychologists must maintain control over the assessment process to protect recipients of neuropsychological services. Vulnerable patient populations are entitled to the greatest protections from potentially harmful services, including services associated with technological advances.

Coverage of ethical issues in neuropsychological assessment would be incomplete without addressing the handling of requests for raw test data from nonpsychologists and the presence of third-party observers. However, because of the extensive coverage that these topics have received in recent years in scholarly publications and presentations, only a brief review is provided here. Interested readers are encouraged to access recent articles and chapters for a more comprehensive review of the ethical, legal, and professional considerations associated with the release of raw test data (e.g., Bush, 2005d; Bush & Lees-Haley, 2005; Bush & Martin, 2006c; Bush, Connell, & Denney, 2006; Erard, 2004; Grote, 2005; Knapp & VandeCreek, 2003b; NAN Policy & Planning Committee, 2000, 2003b; Rapp, Ferber, & Bush, forthcoming) and third-party observers (e.g., American Academy of Clinical Neuropsychology, 2001; Bush, Connell, & Denney, 2006; McCaffrey, 2005; NAN, 2000).

The National Academy of Neuropsychology position papers provide excellent guidance for neuropsychologists interested in concise overviews of the issues and specific directions for handling requests to release raw test data to nonpsychologists or to have neuropsychological evaluations observed. The special issue of the *Journal of Forensic Neuropsychology* edited by McCaffrey (2005) provides an excellent update on the potential effects of observers on test performance. The Bush, Connell, and Denney (2006) test addresses both issues in the context of forensic psychology.

Controversy exists with regard to how to best handle requests from nonpsychologists for raw test data. Failure to maintain the security of test materials can result in misuse, misinterpretation, and harmful effects. However, an obligation also exists to respect the rights of clients (e.g., patients, attorneys) to choose when and to whom records are to be released. Balancing these competing ethical obligations as well as legal requirements in the context of one's practice is needed to arrive at the appropriate course of action.

> It is typically easiest to simply copy and send raw test data upon request, and ethical and legal justification can be found for such an approach. In contrast, general bioethical principles, most ethical and professional guidelines, and federal copyright law support the notion that the security of psychological and neuropsychological tests, including raw test data, must be maintained. (Bush & Martin, 2006c)

Options for responding to requests for raw test data fall on a continuum. The step-by-step decision-making procedure for handling requests for raw test data that has been proposed by the NAN Policy and Planning Committee (2000) is recommended.

The issue of allowing a third party into the neuropsychological evaluation setting is complicated. In some situations, such as with small children or when interpreters are needed, the third party may facilitate performance of the evaluation. In addition, observation is needed for neuropsychological trainees. However, interest in having evaluations observed often arises in the context of litigation, ostensibly motivated by a desire to ensure that the examinee receives an appropriate evaluation, although intimidation of the examiner may also be a goal of the party requesting the observation. Regardless of motives, the presence of the observer may compromise the validity of the test results. Research indicates that both direct observation and indirect observation through recording devices may affect neuropsychological test performance (Constantinou, Ashendorf, & McCaffrey, 2005).

Allowing a third party into the evaluation room represents a deviation from standardized administration, may threaten test security depending on the nature of the observer, and will have unknown effects on the examinee and the validity of the test data. The position of the NAN Policy and Planning Committee (2000) is as follows: "Neuropsychologists should strive to minimize all influences that may compromise accuracy of assessment and should make every effort to exclude observers from the evaluation" (p. 380). Careful consideration should be given to the advantages and disadvantages of allowing deviations from standardized evaluation procedures. If a third party is allowed to observe a neuropsychological evaluation, the neuropsychologist should provide a detailed description of the observer's behavior and the apparent effects, if any, on the examinee, test data, and conclusions.

Learning Exercises

1. What percentage of neuropsychologists' professional time is spent weekly on assessment activities? (*Hint:* You will likely need to review the article by Sweet et al. [2002], which is available online at www.nanonline.org/paio/PaioResLinks .shtm.)

2. Describe potential problems associated with Internet-based test administration and interpretation.

3. What should you do if you receive a request for records, including raw test data, in the form of a subpoena (not a court order)? (*Hint:* See www.nanonline.org/paio/secappend.shtm.)

4. List three reasons why it is not advisable to allow third parties to observe neuropsychological evaluations.

II

▪ ▪ ▪

Therapy

Although assessment is the primary professional activity of clinical neuro-psychologists, many also provide treatment. Psychotherapy with patients that do not have brain dysfunction is the second most prominent clinical activity, in terms of number of hours per week (4.86 hours), for neuropsychologists (Sweet, Grote, & van Gorp, 2002). Neuropsychologists as a group spend approximately 2.70 hours per week providing psychotherapy to patients with acquired brain dysfunction and spend the fewest number of clinical hours per week (0.64 hour) performing cognitive rehabilitation, with 81.3% of the survey respondents performing no cognitive rehabilitation, 9% performing 1–2 hours per week, and 6.6% providing 3–6 hours per week (Sweet, Grote, & van Gorp, 2002). Although considerable overlap exists between ethical requirements of neuropsychologists when conducting evaluations and providing treatment (e.g., competence, informed consent), some ethical issues are unique to or encountered differently in treatment contexts.

Cognitive Rehabilitation

Cognitive rehabilitation is a

> systematic, functionally oriented service of therapeutic activities intended to improve cognitive functioning through (1) reestab-lishing previously learned patterns of behavior; (2) establishing new patterns of cognitive activity through compensatory cognitive mechanisms for impaired neurological systems; (3) establishing new patterns of activity through external compensatory mechanisms or environmental support; and/or (4) enabling persons to adapt to their cognitive disability in order to improve their overall level of functioning and quality of life. (Cicerone et al., 2005)

In their review of the literature on the efficacy of cognitive rehabilitation, Cicerone and colleges (2005) concluded, "There is substantial evidence to support cognitive rehabilitation for people with TBI, including strategy training for mild memory impairment, strategy training for postacute attention deficits, and interventions for functional communication deficits" (p. 1681). In addition, in a position paper on cognitive rehabilitation, the National Academy of Neuropsychology (2002) Policy and Planning Committee concluded, "Most importantly, the last several decades have created a clinical and empirical foundation to provide patients with effective cognitive rehabilitation interventions to promote neurobehavioral recovery and to improve opportunities for returning to productive lives." With the establishment of certain types of cognitive rehabilitation as beneficial for patients with certain neurocognitive deficits and functional limitations, neuropsychologists who provide such rehabilitation or work in multidisciplinary contexts in which other health care professionals are providing the treatment must be aware of relevant ethical issues.

CASE 11.1

A neuropsychologist who recently transitioned from performing evaluations on an epilepsy unit to consulting in a skilled nursing facility (SNF) performs a brief neuropsychological evaluation of a 28-year-old woman who is 2 years post–severe traumatic brain injury. Based on findings of severe impairment with attention, memory, and processing speed, the clinician begins cognitive rehabilitation. Three times per week, the neuropsychologist brings a laptop computer into the patient's room, sets up a series of computer-based mental exercises, helps the patient begin the exercises, and then leaves the room to see other patients.

As with all professional services, neuropsychologists must have the education, training, and experience necessary to perform cognitive rehabilitation competently (ES 2.01, Boundaries of Competence) or be actively pursuing competence through appropriate training or consultation (ES 2.01d). The neuropsychologist in this case appears to lack competence in cognitive rehabilitation and was not pursuing the needed education and skills. Although there exists a need for expanded educational opportunities in neurorehabilitation for neuropsychology graduate students (Uzzell, 2000), neuropsychologists must not engage in cognitive rehabilitation unless they are competent to do so.

Although the patient in this vignette may have benefited from certain types of compensatory strategies designed to improve autonomy and quality of life within the SNF setting, she was unlikely to benefit from unsupervised computer-based mental exercises.

Ethical Standard 10.10, Terminating Therapy

(a) Psychologists terminate therapy when it becomes reasonably clear that the client/patient no longer needs the service, is not likely to benefit, or is being harmed by continued service.

Neuropsychologists who perform treatment, including cognitive rehabilitation, should adopt an evidence-based approach and attempt to match interventions with patient and injury characteristics. In this case, the neuropsychologist should have known that this patient would be unlikely to benefit from the intended intervention. Establishing unrealistic expectations for the patient and her family may cause undue disappointment when the patient fails to demonstrate improved neurocognitive functioning (ES 10.01, Informed Consent to Therapy; ES 3.04, Avoiding Harm). Additionally, the neuropsychologist is probably committing fraud by billing for individual treatment without maintaining face-to-face interaction.

CASE 11.2

A neuropsychologist performs an evaluation and begins treating a 42-year-old man who sustained an electrical brain injury. After two months of treatment, the neuropsychologist learns that the patient has begun receiving psychotherapy from a clinical psychologist at a nearby clinic. The neuropsychologist informs the patient that he is ethically prohibited from treating someone who is in treatment with another psychologist and asks the patient to choose between neuropsychological treatment and psychotherapy.

■ ■ ■

Ethical Standard 10.04, Providing Therapy to Those Served by Others

In deciding whether to offer or provide services to those already receiving mental health services elsewhere, psychologists carefully consider the treatment issues and the potential client's/patient's welfare. Psychologists discuss these issues with the client/patient or another legally authorized person on behalf of the client/patient in order to minimize the risk of confusion and conflict, consult with the other service providers when appropriate, and proceed with caution and sensitivity to the therapeutic issues.

In this case the neuropsychologist appears to have misunderstood his ethical obligation. ES 10.04 does not prohibit a clinician from providing treatment to a patient simply because the patient is receiving services from another clinician. In fact, because of the uniqueness and potentially complimentary nature of the different services provided in this case, treatment by both clinicians may be preferred. The neuropsychologist should have discussed with the patient the need for coordination of services, requested permission to contact and communicate with the psychotherapist to coordinate services, and proceeded with the patient's best interests in mind.

An inappropriate discharge could be considered abandonment. Even though the patient was in treatment with a clinical psychologist, neuropsychological services were deemed medically necessary by the neuropsychologist. Abruptly ending needed treatment without facilitating a transition to another neuropsychologist would represent ethical misconduct and could result in a complaint to an ethics or state licensing board or a malpractice suit (Knapp & VandeCreek, 2006). "The four Ds of malpractice suits are the presence of a duty, the deviation from the standards of the profession, damage to the patient, and the direct connection between the deviation from duty and the damage to the patient" (p. 197). Although these four criteria for malpractice suits may not have been met in this case, it is advisable to discuss termination issues with patients and present them with options as soon as it becomes apparent that services are no longer beneficial or must be terminated for another reason (e.g., denial of insurance coverage).

Psychological Treatment

Some neuropsychologists provide psychotherapy for patients without brain dysfunction who represent the full range of life challenges and psychiatric disorders. Ethical issues related to clinical psychological treatments have been addressed in detail in general psychology ethics publications (e.g., Knapp & VandeCreek, 2006; Koocher & Keith-Spiegel, 1998; Nagy, 2000)

Psychological treatment of persons with neurological injury or illness who experience emotional adjustment problems, posttraumatic stress, or other psychological disorders may occur as individual psychotherapy, group or family therapy, or a component of a more comprehensive intervention that includes cognitive rehabilitation.

CASE 11.3

A 16-year-old girl was recently struck by a car while riding her bicycle, sustaining a moderate traumatic brain injury and multiple facial abrasions and lacerations. She begins neuropsychological treatment, which consists of learning compensatory strategies to help with her transition back to school, as well as psychotherapy to maximize her emotional adjustment, particularly given her feelings of being unattractive and different and her fear of becoming isolated from peers. Treatment begins well. After one session the neuropsychologist finds the patient's mother crying in the waiting room. The mother is invited into the office and expresses her own emotional reactions to her daughter's injuries and changes. The neuropsychologist offers empathic and supportive statements and then discusses the patient's therapy. The patient listens, surprised, as the neuropsychologist then conveys very personal and sensitive information that she thought was confidential. The patient feels betrayed and refuses to return for therapy.

Ethical Standard 10.02, Therapy Involving Couples or Families

(a) When psychologists agree to provide services to several persons who have a relationship (such as spouses, significant others, or parents and children), they take reasonable steps to clarify at the outset (1) which of the individuals are clients/patients and (2) the relationship the psychologist will have with each person. This clarification includes the psychologist's role and the probable uses of the services provided or the information obtained.

The neuropsychologist blurred the treatment boundaries and may have failed to maintain confidentiality (ES 4.01, Maintaining Confidentiality; ES 4.02, Discussing the Limits of Confidentiality; ES 4.05, Disclosures), although it is unclear whether the patient forgot the limits to confidentiality that were established when therapy began. Autonomy management is often an important aspect of the treatment of patients with neurological dysfunction. Adolescents, older adults, and others often struggle to achieve and maintain autonomy. Engaging patients in the informed consent process to the extent possible and periodically reviewing information presented during the consent process demonstrates the therapist's respect for patient autonomy, often strengthens the therapeutic alliance, and may remind all parties of the treatment parameters and confidentiality requirements.

Neuropsychologists who evaluate or treat competent adults for whom significant neurocognitive dysfunction or deterioration is anticipated have an opportunity (and perhaps obligation) to determine the patient's thoughts and feelings about information that is relevant for advance directives. In addition to being qualified to determine decision-making capacity, neuropsychologists are well suited to assess a patient's values history. In contrast to traditional advance directive, the values history gives a picture of the patient as an individual person rather than as a set of medical paradigms, emphasizing autonomy (Doukas & McCullough, 1991). When taking a values history, the clinician elicits information about the patient's lifestyle, attitudes, and preferences regarding the states of health a patient would find acceptable and options for maintaining or declining aggressive treatment and comfort care.[1]

---

[1] A values history form is available online from the University of New Mexico Institute for Ethics at hsc.unm.edu/ethics/advdir/vhform_eng.shtml.

Ethical Decision Making in Clinical Neuropsychology

The existence of a values history allows decision makers to better understand the nature of a patient's wishes regarding quality of life when the patient no longer has the capacity to make decisions and explain the rationale and spirit behind decisions relevant to treatment and care options. This information can be particularly valuable in situations that are not always addressed in traditional advance directives, such as minimally conscious states.

Health Promotion

The preservation of youth and youthful health has been a primary goal throughout history. With biomedical and technological advances in recent years, the attainment of these goals is drawing ever closer. Increasing life expectancy is evidence that these advances have already had some success. Preservation of neurological health and neurocognitive functioning is an important aspect of the pursuit of longevity.

In addition to preserving health and functioning, many people are invested in enhancing appearance and normal performance. Cosmetic surgery and use of performance-enhancing drugs are two examples of ways that physically healthy people address the real or perceived limitations of their genetics. Enhanced neurological performance is at least equally desirable for many people.

The enhancement of healthy or normal neurological functioning has a long history. For example, it is likely that most readers of this text have used caffeine to improve or maintain alertness and vigilance while studying or working. Similarly, many truck drivers, pilots, students, and others use over-the-counter, prescribed, or illicit stimulants to maintain wakefulness and alertness and to improve their performance. Researchers are working on developing and refining biotechnological procedures to directly improve neurocognitive functioning in neurologically healthy individuals, yet practical and ethical guidelines governing their use are only just emerging (Bush, 2006).

CASE 11.4

A neuropsychologist's caseload includes two college seniors being treated for anxiety stemming from concerns about graduation and their futures. One of the patients sustained a moderate TBI in an extreme sports competition in the fall semester. Both are preparing to take the GRE so that they can pursue graduate education, and both are interested in enhancing their alertness and ability to focus when taking the exam. The neuropsychologist provides general information regarding test-taking strategies. She also refers both patients to a psychiatrist whom she knows will prescribe modafinil, which has been found to improve arousal and attention in healthy adults to the extent of being included on the World Anti-Doping Agency's list of banned substances because of the unfair advantage its use provides athletes.

It is common for patients with brain dysfunction to ask neuropsychologists about options for improving neurocognitive functioning, and it is professionally and ethically appropriate and necessary for neuropsychologists to provide education about evidence-based treatment options. The Ethics Code provides information regarding treatments for which supporting evidence has not yet been established.

Ethical Standard 10.01, Informed Consent to Therapy

(b) When obtaining informed consent for treatment for which generally recognized techniques and procedures have not been established, psychologists inform their clients/patients of the developing nature of the treatment, the potential risks involved, alternative treatments that may be available, and the voluntary nature of their participation.

One problematic aspect of this standard in the context of emerging biotechnological options is that not all potential risks may be known or anticipated. The adverse effects of a new drug or surgical procedure may not become widely known until numerous people have been harmed. Although most neuropsychologists do not prescribe medications or perform surgical procedures, it is not uncommon for them to counsel individuals who are considering such options. As biotechnological advances continue and consumers become increasingly aware of the advances, neuropsychologists must be prepared to field questions about neurocognitive enhancement options.

A 65-year-old woman reads in the newspaper that blueberries and crossword puzzles help prevent Alzheimer's disease, and she is interested in obtaining more information because her mother developed "hardening of the arteries" in her seventies and she would like to avoid such a fate if possible. She contacts her primary care physician, is prescribed donepezil prophylactically, and is referred to a neuropsychologist to address the "use-it-or-lose-it" aspect of her neurocognitive health. The neuropsychologist informs the woman that promising research has emerged in the past few years indicating that people who engage in mentally stimulating activities, including computer-based neurocognitive exercises, have a significantly reduced chance of developing Alzheimer's disease. He describes his proposed neurocognitive stimulation program, which mirrors one of the research protocols; he cautions the patient about possible adverse effects, such as frustration with computerized exercises or disappointment due to unrealistic expectations; he also states that he could not bill her insurance because the program is not considered treatment per se. She understands the information and begins the neurocognitive enhancement program.

Some neuropsychologists may choose to develop practices devoted to the cosmetic neuropsychology—that is, meeting the needs of healthy individuals seeking to improve their neurocognitive functioning and their perceived quality of life (Bush, 2006). The clinician in this case is providing professional consultation but not treatment. As a result, sections of the Ethics Code that pertain to human relations (ES 3) may be more relevant than sections related to treatment (ES 10). In addition, because neurocognitive enhancement is an emerging subspecialty, it is not specifically addressed in existing professional guidelines, requiring practitioners to examine and balance underlying bioethical principles when considering such services. The neuropsychologist carefully explained the potential benefits and risks of the proposed neurocognitive enhancement program, including taking care to not have the consumer establish unrealistic expectations, and ensured that the consumer possessed the information necessary to make an informed choice about participation.

> Facilitating an individual's pursuit of self-betterment certainly appears to be consistent with ethical practice, but beneficence requires consideration of the strength of the evidence of benefit and the potential risks. While the need to assist recipients of neuropsychological services is a primary professional obligation, the greater responsibility is to limit to the extent possible detrimental actions (General Principle A). (Bush, 2006, p. 128)

Many healthy people now use enhancing products to maintain smooth skin, manage daily stressors, maintain erections, and promote physical ability, among other things; neurocognitive enhancement will not be left out of the self-improvement movement (Bush, 2006). Nonpharmacologic and noninvasive methods, such as computer-based neurocognitive exercise programs, provide a safe means of potentially maximizing neurocognitive health (Ball et al., 2002; Kramer et al., 2004) and sense of self-control (Bush & Martin, 2004). Neuropsychologists who anticipate fielding questions from consumers about enhancement options or are considering entering this emerging area of practice have an obligation to pursue or endorse only those practices that reflect the best interests of consumers and society (Bush, 2006).

Learning Exercises

1. Describe ethical issues that must be considered when providing (or supervising others who provide) cognitive rehabilitation.

2. Describe primary ethical issues that emerge in the treatment of children and adolescents. What makes the ethical considerations in the treatment of minors differ from that of adults?

3. In case 11.4, should the neuropsychologist have handled the two patients differently? Explain your reasoning.

4. Describe one primary ethical challenge associated with the use of new treatment options.

12

■ ■ ■

Addressing Ethical Misconduct

Though I am not naturally honest, I am so sometimes by chance.

—Autolycus,
in William Shakespeare, *Winter's Tale*, act 4, scene 4

All neuropsychologists who engage in forensic activities and many whose practices are strictly clinical are aware of colleagues who appear to be incompetent, biased, incompetent *and* biased, or in some other way unethical some if not most of the time. Of course, those colleagues may think the same things about us. Shakespeare's Autolycus at least acknowledges his moral flaws, if only to himself. Although few of us likely see ourselves as generally unethical, no one is immune from behavior that others may find ethically questionable.

CASE 12.1

Dr. A is retained by a no-fault insurance carrier to review Dr. B's neuropsychological report and bill for the purpose of determining whether the evaluation was medically necessary and the bill appropriate. Dr. B's patient was involved in a relatively minor motor vehicle accident, with no apparent loss of consciousness or posttraumatic amnesia, and is involved in litigation. The information obtained by Dr. A indicates that Dr. B performed 12 hours of neuropsychological testing over the course of 2 days, 1 month after the patient's accident. He also billed for two hours of clinical interview, performed on the day after the testing was completed. Dr. A concludes that medical necessity for the 12 hours of testing had not been established and, had Dr. B performed the clinical interview prior to the testing, he would have known that testing was unnecessary. Dr. A recommends that Dr. B be paid for one hour of clinical interview time only. When Dr. B receives a copy of Dr. A's report with the explanation of benefits summary, he contacts Dr. A, states that Dr. A has violated Ethical Standard 9.01 (Bases for Assessments). Dr. B claims that Dr. A arrived at inappropriate conclusions because he did not evaluate the patient in person. Dr. B states that Dr. A should consider their conversation an attempt at an informal resolution of the matter, and if Dr. A does not contact the no-fault carrier and change his recommendation, a formal ethics complaint will be forthcoming. Dr. B directs Dr. A to the relevant sections of the Ethics Code.[1]

Ethical Standard 1.04, Informal Resolution of Ethical Violations

When psychologists believe that there may have been an ethical violation by another psychologist, they attempt to resolve the issue by bringing it to the attention of that individual, if an informal resolution appears appropriate and the intervention does not violate any confidentiality rights that may be involved.

Ethical Standard 1.05, Reporting Ethical Violations

If an apparent ethical violation has substantially harmed or is likely to substantially harm a person or organization and is not appropriate for informal resolution under Standard 1.04, Informal

---

[1] In the APA Ethics Code, the section on resolving ethical issues was moved from the last section (Standard 8) in the 1992 code to the first section (Standard 1) in the 2002 code. This change appears to reflect increased importance being placed on the appropriate resolution of ethical issues; however, knowledge of the ethical issues and requirements seems necessary before considering how to resolve them.

Ethical Decision Making in Clinical Neuropsychology

Resolution of Ethical Violations, or is not resolved properly in that fashion, psychologists take further action appropriate to the situation. Such action might include referral to state or national committees on professional ethics, to state licensing boards, or to the appropriate institutional authorities. This standard does not apply when an intervention would violate confidentiality rights or when psychologists have been retained to review the work of another psychologist whose professional conduct is in question.

Dr. A, somewhat surprised that he is being accused of ethical misconduct, directs Dr. B to subsection (c) of ES 9.01, which states the following.

When psychologists conduct a record review or provide consultation or supervision and an individual examination is not warranted or necessary for the opinion, psychologists explain this and the sources of information on which they based their conclusions and recommendations.

Dr. A states that his practices in this case were consistent with the ethical requirements and that if Dr. B persists with his accusations, he will find himself the subject of an ethics complaint. Dr. A does not hear anything else about the matter and continues to approach record reviews the same way he did in this case.

At some point, with more or less frequency depending on practice context, most neuropsychologists will likely observe behavior of colleagues that they perceive to ethically inappropriate. When such observations are made, neuropsychologists must determine whether to address the behavior and if so, how and when. These tend to be among the most difficult decisions faced by neuropsychologists and should not be made without due consideration of the nature of and circumstances surrounding the apparent misconduct. Previous publications have proposed steps to take to facilitate the decision-making process (Bush, Connell, & Denney, 2006; Deidan & Bush, 2002; Grote, Lewin, Sweet, & van Gorp, 2000; Koocher & Keith-Spiegel, 1998; Martelli, Bush, & Zasler, 2003).

The steps in the ethical decision-making model presented in chapter 3 cover much of the content of these models. However, depending on the situation, the following factors may also need to be considered: (1) the context, especially as it pertains to patient confidentiality or ongoing litigation;

(2) the significance of the violation; (3) personal feelings toward the colleague; (4) possible mandated actions; (5) the timing of any action to address the misconduct; and (6) the potential for counteraction by the colleague. Timing can be particularly important in situations in which the possibility of considerable harm exists and in the context of ongoing litigation.

Clearly, if a colleague's actions are resulting in or have a high likelihood of causing substantial harm to others, action should be taken relatively quickly. In contrast, perceived ethical misconduct in the context of litigation, unless substantial physical harm is likely, may require patience on the part of the observer to avoid the perception that allegations of ethical misconduct were made as a tactic to discredit an opposing expert. Using allegations of ethical misconduct as a litigation tactic is unprofessional and unethical (AACN, 2003; ES 1.07, Improper Complaints). Sweet and colleagues offered the following general guideline, "If ethical concerns that arise *within* a forensic context remain salient *after* the case has been concluded, then it is appropriate to consider whether any action is necessary" (Sweet, Grote, & van Gorp, 2002, p. 55). However, a complication arises when multiple cases overlap between colleagues and span many years, and the apparently offending colleague's behavior remains unaddressed and inappropriate. Macartney-Filgate (in Bush et al., 2007) noted the bind in which neuropsychologists may find themselves when facing ethical challenges in the context of litigation: "It is not appropriate to risk prejudicing any case, but at the same time one cannot avoid the issue if doing nothing poses a risk of harm to the interests of the assessed party and/or client, or to other individuals being assessed by the same practitioner."

In addition to performing a cost-benefit analysis to help determine the preferable course of action, it is advisable to seek input from objective, knowledgeable colleagues, ethics committees, the state licensing board, one's professional liability insurance carrier, or one's own attorney. It is also important to document each step taken prior to taking (or electing not to take) action to address a colleague's apparent ethical misconduct.

Smith and colleagues (1991) found that even when psychologists go through an appropriate decision-making process and determine a course of action that is needed to address colleague's misconduct, they are ultimately more likely to base their actions or inactions on their own values and practicalities. The personal unpleasantness and risk of counteraction are hurdles that some neuropsychologists cannot overcome when confronted with ethical misconduct of colleagues. However, neuropsychology will continue to progress and remain a viable and respected specialty only if we make personal commitments to pursue high ethical standards and address ethical misconduct when it is encountered.

Learning Exercise

1. Use the ethical decision-making model presented in chapter 3 and the six additional considerations presented here to arrive at an appropriate course of action for Dr. D in the following case.

   Dr. C is frequently retained by defense counsel in civil litigation cases and, in Dr. D's opinion, his conclusions are always the same—that there is no evidence of traumatic brain injury and the litigant is presenting with implausible symptoms that likely reflect dissimulation. In fact, Dr. C's conclusions appear to be established prior to performing the evaluations. Dr. D struggles to accept Dr. C's conclusions as simply representing a difference of opinion based on a different understanding of the neuropsychological literature and different professional experiences. In fact, they have discussed their differences of opinion in general terms on a professional online discussion list. However, on one occasion, Dr. C examines one of Dr. D's patients who Dr. D knows to have sustained significant trauma, including a mild traumatic brain injury, in a motor vehicle accident, with devastating effects on the patient's life. Dr. C appeared to have administered every published symptom validity test, the scores for a couple of which fell in a range suggestive of invalid responding. Dr. C concluded that Dr. D's patient was malingering, and the evaluation results were used to deny disability benefits, placed the patient's lawsuit in serious jeopardy of being dismissed, and caused the patient to become suicidal. Dr. D felt that Dr. C's opinions no longer simply reflected a difference of opinion but were intentionally biased and very harmful to the patient. Dr. D wonders what steps to take to address what he perceives to be ethical misconduct.

13

■ ■ ■

A Complex Case

Although some very complex and ethically challenging situations involve only one clinical conflict that pits two ethical principles against each other, some situations, as illustrated by case 13.1, involve a host of ethical conflicts or violations, some of which are immediately evident and others that are more subtle. In situations in which multiple ethical problems exist, the most obvious problems are not necessarily the most egregious. Subtle problems, because they may be overlooked among the more obvious ones, may go unaddressed, with harmful results, for longer periods of time. Therefore, when confronted with ethical problems in their own practices or the practices of colleagues, neuropsychologists should carefully examine the surrounding circumstances for additional contributing problems that should also be addressed.

CASE 13.1

Dr. A, a psychologist on an adult inpatient brain injury rehabilitation unit, is told to provide coverage for Dr. B, the neuropsychologist on the pediatric unit who is on vacation. Dr. A agrees and goes to the unit with his usual tests because he does not have access to Dr. B's office where the pediatric tests are kept. However, sensitive to the fact that the tests to which he has access were not normed with children, he is determined to score them qualitatively and interpret them with caution.

The first patient to be evaluated is a 12-year-old bilingual (Spanish-English) boy who sustained a severe TBI 4 weeks prior. Dr. A performs the evaluation, including testing, bedside. The patient's mother remains in his room to help encourage and reassure him and to interpret instructions and responses if needed. During administration of the Trail Making Test (TMT), the patient states, "This one is fun. I like doing it in OT." The patient's roommate adds that he likes it, too. The roommate then agrees to remain quiet for the rest of the evaluation, but his physical therapist soon comes and takes him for therapy anyway. Dr. A completes the evaluation and writes his brief report in the patient's chart. Dr. Z, a colleague of Dr. A, working in a different department in the same facility, learns of this situation.

Learning Exercise

1. Before proceeding to the case analysis, list the ethical problems that you can identify in this case.
2. List the APA Ethical Standards that apply to the ethical problems that you have identified.

Case Analysis

The ethical decision-making model is approached somewhat differently depending on whether the practitioner is confronting an ethical dilemma and needs direction or has already engaged in ethically inappropriate conduct that must be addressed for professional growth or punishment. In either scenario, the same decision-making steps are applied. For case 13.1, the action has already occurred, and Dr. J is considering the problems and the steps she should take. The model is applied case 13.1 as follows.

Identify the Problem(s) or Dilemma(s)

Dr. Z identifies five general ethical problems, each with more specific violations that are described in greater detail the Ethical and Legal Resources section. First, Dr. A allowed himself to be put in a situation that he was not qualified to handle and therefore mishandled, to the detriment of the patient and others. He is a psychologist but not a neuropsychologist. He should not perform neuropsychological services without the necessary education, training, and experience to do so competently. Furthermore, he usually works with adults and is not qualified to work with pediatric populations.

Second, Dr. A performed an inappropriate evaluation that would likely have multiple adverse repercussions. He used adult tests with a child and did not appear to consider the potential impact of the patient's ethnicity, cultural background, or English language fluency on the tests selected or the validity of the results. There was a complete lack of scientific evidence to support any conclusions Dr. A may have drawn from his evaluation.

Third, Dr. A failed to adequately manage aspects of practice that he would have been expected to manage in any context, such as the testing environment and linguistic issues. Dr. A did not appear to have taken steps to maximize privacy and confidentiality during the evaluation, and he performed the evaluation with others in the room. In addition, he used the patient's mother as an interpreter, although her ability to provide accurate interpretation and do so objectively with her child was unknown but unlikely. Any consent that he obtained from the patient and his mother could not have been based on an informed decision; Dr. A could not have appropriately informed them of the risks because he was apparently unaware of at least some of them himself and dismissed the rest as not sufficiently important to prohibit the evaluation.

Fourth, in addition to his own mistakes, Dr. A learned that other health care professionals were misusing neuropsychological instruments, possibly with the knowledge of Dr. B. The occupational therapist apparently used the TMT as a therapeutic exercise on a regular basis. Dr. B, who regularly worked on the unit must have been aware of the OT's practice and either supported, or did not adequately oppose, the practice. Fifth, problematic institutional or departmental practices emerged, such as not providing appropriate neuropsychological coverage during Dr. B's vacation and pressuring Dr. A into providing services he was not qualified to perform.

Consider the Significance of the Context and Setting
The setting is significant in this case. Dr. Z realizes that the ethical problems begin with the facility not providing coverage for Dr. B's vacation with a neuropsychologist who was competent to perform the work that is required on the pediatric unit. Because of a lack of appropriate coverage, Dr. A was

asked or told to provide services that are outside his areas of competence. The extent to which the facility would have been responsive had Dr. A expressed concerns about performing the services and suggested other options, such as retaining an outside pediatric neuropsychologist, was not addressed in the vignette. The interdisciplinary nature of the setting may have contributed to the occupational therapist obtaining and using a neuropsychological test for treatment, apparently without Dr. B addressing the issue. The setting was also significant because physical trauma may have required the patient to be evaluated bedside, despite having a roommate. The setting also allowed for a physical therapist to enter the room and remove the patient's roommate during testing. Additionally, Dr. A's access to an appropriate interpreter at the time of the evaluation is unknown.

Identify and Utilize Ethical and Legal Resources
Related to the 5 general ethical problems, Dr. Z identifies more than 20 APA Ethical Standards and Principles were violated. In addition, the SEPT and position papers of professional organizations are applicable.

First and foremost, Dr. A overstepped the boundaries of his competence on multiple levels (ES 2.01, Boundaries of Competence; SEPT 11.3 and 12.1). Although Dr. A may have believed that he was justified in overstepping these boundaries because there was no one more qualified to provide the service and the patient was in need of a neuropsychological evaluation (ES 2.02, Providing Services in Emergencies), he would have needed to carefully weigh the possible advantages against the possible risks by examining additional Ethical Standards and Principles. It is unlikely that he could justify going beyond his own competence as he did.

Second, Dr. A performed an inappropriate evaluation. He selected and administered tests that were completely unsuitable, and any clinical opinions that he based on his evaluation lacked scientific support and were thus invalid and potential harmful to the patient (Ethical Standards 9.01, Bases for Assessments; 9.02, Use of Assessments; 9.06, Interpreting Assessment Results; 2.04 Bases for Scientific and Professional Judgments; SEPT Standards 7.10, 11.4, and 12.13).

Third, Dr. A did not maintain sufficient control over the evaluation setting. Privacy and confidentiality were not maintained (ES 4.01, Maintaining Confidentiality; HIPAA; SEPT Standard 11.14), which likely adversely affected the patient's test performance but also, perhaps more important, placed the patient in a potentially embarrassing or demeaning position by highlighting his weaknesses in front of his roommate (GP E, Respect for People's Rights and Dignity). Additionally, other staff members entered and left the room during the evaluation, which could also adversely affect test performance and the patient's feelings of privacy and security, which may limit his ability to speak openly and honestly about personal, emotion-laden issues (ES 4.04, Minimizing Intrusions on Privacy). The inclusion of others in the room during the evaluation also threatened test security (ES 9.11, Maintaining Test Security; SEPT 11.7), the validity of the examinee's test results (had appropriate tests been used), and the validity of the roommate's performance during subsequent testing. Appropriate informed consent could not be obtained because Dr. A did not realized or appreciate the significance of the risks inherent in his evaluation (ES 3.10, Informed Consent; ES 9.03, Informed Consent in Assessments; ES 4.02, Discussing the Limits of Confidentiality; SEPT Standard 12.10).

Fourth, Dr. A found out that an occupational therapist was inappropriately using at least one neuropsychological test as a therapeutic activity, which could invalidate the subsequent neuropsychological evaluation results of some patients (ES 9.07, Assessment by Unqualified Persons). Dr. A has an obligation to not only take stops to have such treatment practices discontinued but also to determine whether Dr. B was aware of and supportive of the practice. If Dr. B had been aware of the OT practice, Dr. A had an obligation to address the relevant ethical concerns with Dr. B (ES 1.04, Informal Resolution of Ethical Violations).

Fifth, Drs. A and B had an obligation to address ethical concerns, such as lack of appropriate vacation coverage and the importance of working only within boundaries of competence, with the program or facility administration (ES 1.03, Conflicts between Ethics and Organizational Demands). They had an obligation to make known their commitment to professional ethics and attempt to resolve these problems in a professionally ethical manner.

Taken together, Dr. Z understands that Dr. A's actions, and possibly Dr. B's as well, resulted in an appropriate evaluation with invalid results and conclusions, which could potentially contribute to harmful decisions about the patient's care, treatment, and discharge plans and would certainly not be beneficial to the patient, his family, or the treatment team (ES 3.04, Avoiding Harm; GP A, Beneficence and Nonmaleficence). Dr. Z continues with her decision-making process.

Consider Personal Beliefs and Values

Dr. Z understands her responsibilities to patients, the public, and the profession, and she feels a particular obligation to protect vulnerable individuals who are not in a good position to advocate for their own needs. She would rather not have to confront colleagues about their inappropriate conduct, but she is willing to do so for the benefit of all involved.

Develop Possible Solutions to the Problem

Dr. Z realizes that she has two primary options: discussing the issues with her colleagues or avoiding the issues. However, she also understands that such a discussion could be handled in a variety of ways, including meeting individually with Drs. A and B or meeting with them together and having solutions to propose to them, rather than just allegations of misconduct. For example, despite the potential for interruptions and limited privacy inherent in their practice setting, Dr. Z can propose that they use "privacy" signs on doors, coordinate with nursing staff to minimize interruptions, and determine the roommate's physical therapy schedule and plan the evaluation while the roommate is not in the room. Whether she chooses to address or avoid the ethical issues, she must ensure that the patient in this case receives an appropriate evaluation.

Consider the Potential Consequences of Various Solutions

If Dr. Z meets with Drs. A and B and discusses her concerns, she may find them to be defensive or upset, which may not only affect her relationship with them but require her to take additional, more formal actions to address the problems. However, if she does not attempt to address her concerns informally with Drs. A and B, similar misconduct would probably continue, and she would be neglecting her responsibility.

Choose and Implement a Course of Action

Dr. Z decides to propose that Drs. A and B meet with her for a brainstorming session about ways to handle various challenges that she has experienced and observed in their institution. She intends to begin by disclosing her own difficulties and then inviting them to do the same. She will then raise any additional issues that are left unaddressed. She will suggest that they develop solutions to the problems that they have encountered or can anticipate. She will ensure that the patient is reevaluated by Dr. B. Although not done before, she will propose that the three of them meet regularly to exchange ideas and experiences and address ongoing challenges.

Assess the Outcome and Implement Changes as Needed

Drs. A and B agree to meet with Dr. Z. The meeting begins well, with Dr. Z "taking minutes" so that they would have documentation of the steps taken to address their practices. Dr. A willingly acknowledged the challenges he faced while covering for Dr. B, felt badly that he had handled the situation poorly, and was invested in working with his colleagues to improve their psychological and neuropsychological services. He acknowledged that the patient needed to be reevaluated by Dr. B.

Dr. B agreed with the need to immediately reevaluate the patient and stated that he would do so; however, he became defensive at the suggestion that he may have neglected his responsibilities by not addressing the OT's use of neuropsychological tests for therapeutic exercises. Given Dr. A's openness to self-examination, he became angry with Dr. B for being unwilling to do the same. Dr. B left the meeting abruptly and expressed animosity toward Drs. A and Z from that point forward. Drs. A and Z worked together to improve their services and held inservices for other disciplines on a variety of neuropsychology-related topics, including educating them about neuropsychological services and the importance of only using neuropsychological tests for the purposes for which they were developed. The other disciplines were very receptive and appreciated the inservices.

Learning Exercises

1. Considering the ethical issues and Ethical Standards that you identified after reading the vignette, describe the similarities and differences between your own analysis of the case and the text analysis based on the ethical decision-making model. That is, did you conceptualize the case differently? If so, in what way(s)?

2. Identify factors that Dr. J should have considered, but apparently did not, when determining how best to address the ethical problems that she discovered. *Hint*: Review chapter 12.

Afterword

Attempting to understand the complexity of the brain and the human experience of persons who present with brain-related concerns can be a daunting goal, one that cannot be achieved without an understanding of the relevant ethical issues and challenges. Ethical challenges in clinical neuropsychology are many and varied. Although considerable overlap exists between the ethical issues relevant to clinical psychology and those that pertain to neuropsychology, unique variations and issues are encountered in neuropsychology. In this book I have described common ethical issues and challenges encountered in neuropsychology, and I have emphasized three main points to facilitate making good decisions regarding professional conduct.

First, neuropsychologists should adopt a positive, proactive approach to ethical, professional conduct. Anticipating ethical challenges that may be encountered in a given practice setting or context, developing strategies for resolving such challenges, and maintaining a personal commitment to pursuing ethical ideals will maximize ethical conduct. Misconduct may be intentional or unintentional, but a personal commitment to pursuing high ethical standards can reduce unintentional misconduct.

Second, neuropsychologists should use an ethical decision-making model to resolve challenges proactively or once they occur. Models such as the one presented herein provide a systematic method of gathering, reviewing, and weighing the information needed for appropriate ethical decision making. Third, neuropsychologists should use multiple professional, ethical, and legal resources, including ethics committees and colleagues, in the decision-making process. The American Psychological Association Ethics Code is the primary ethical resource for neuropsychologists and should typically be the first resource reviewed when anticipating or confronting ethical challenges; however, it is essential to consult additional resources, including colleagues, when the Ethics Code does not provide the necessary guidance or when confronting an ethical dilemma (i.e., when two or more ethical principles conflict).

As clinical neuropsychology continues to develop and evolve, so will neuropsychological ethics. Neuropsychologists invested in pursuing high ethical standards will continue to serve consumers and the profession well and will likely achieve much satisfaction from their work.

Appendix A

Excerpt from "The Oral Examination: Professional and Ethical Issues" (McSweeny, 2002)

The candidate will be given the vignette with the potential ethical conflicts and allowed to read it for approximately five minutes. The candidate is welcome to take notes while reading the vignette in order to help analyze the issues, identify the relevant standards from the APA Ethics Code and organize his/her presentation to the examiner. Any notes taken will be collected at the end of this section of the examination.

After the candidate has finished reading the vignette, he or she will be asked to identify and discuss the ethical issues in it. The candidate will be asked to identify the relevant standards from the Ethics Code. He or she *does not* need to know the numbers associated with the Ethical Standards or be able to quote them verbatim. However, the candidate should be able to describe the concepts involved in the Standards and discuss how they apply to the situation or vignette, in other words, answering the question, "Just what are the (ethical) problems here?" The discussion of the Ethics Code should include an explanation of the reasoning behind them. The ABCN is aware that parts of the current Ethics Code are controversial, and if the candidate wishes to note disagreement with the principles, he or she should feel free to do so, as long as he or she can explain the position with respect to the intent of the Principle and why he or she believes it is flawed.

In addition to being able to identify and discuss the parts of the Ethics Code inherent in the situation described in the vignette, the candidate should be able to discuss how the situation might be handled differently. The candidate should ask him or herself, "What would I do in this situation to resolve it in an ethical fashion?" Be ready to discuss solutions as well as problems. (p. 68)

Appendix B

Neuropsychology-Related Ethics References

Books

American Educational Research Association, American Psychological Association, National Council on measurement in Education (1999). *Standards for educational and psychological testing*. Washington, DC: American Educational Research Association.

Beauchamp, T. L., & Childress, J. F. (2001). *Principles of biomedical ethics* (5th ed.). New York: Oxford University Press.

Bush, S. S., ed. (2005). *A casebook of ethical challenges in neuropsychology*. New York: Psychology Press.

Bush, S. S., Connell, M. A., & Denney, R. L. (2006). *Ethical practice in forensic psychology: A systematic model for decision making*. Washington, DC: American Psychological Association.

Bush, S. S., & Drexler, M. L., eds. (2002). *Ethical issues in clinical neuropsychology*. Lisse, Netherlands: Swets & Zeitlinger.

Fletcher-Janzen, E., Strickland, L., & Reynolds, C., eds. (2000). *Handbook of cross-cultural neuropsychology*. New York: Kluwer Academic/Plenum Publishers.

Grisso, T., & Appelbaum, P. (1998). *Assessing competence to consent to treatment: A guide for physicians and other health professionals*. New York: Oxford University Press.

Hanson, S., Kerkhoff, T., & Bush, S. (2005). *Health care ethics for psychologists: A casebook*. Washington, DC: American Psychological Association.

Heilbrun, K. (2001). *Principles of forensic mental health assessment*. New York: Kluwer Academic/Plenum Publishers.

Nell, V. (2000). *Cross-cultural neuropsychological assessment: Theory and practice*. Mahway, NJ: Erlbaum.

Samuda, R. J. (1998). *Psychological testing of American minorities: Issues and consequences, second edition.* Thousand Oaks, CA: Sage.

Sandoval, C. L., Frisby, K. F., Geisinger, J. D., et al., eds. (1998). *Test interpretation and diversity: Achieving equity in assessment.* Washington DC: American Psychological Association.

Special Journal Issues

Banja, J. D., ed. (1989). Ethical and legal issues. *Journal of Head Trauma Rehabilitation, 4* (1).

Banja, J. D., & Rosenthal, M. (guest editors) (1996). Ethics. *NeuroRehabilitation, 6* (2), special issue.

Bush, S. S. (guest editor) (2005). Ethical issues in forensic neuropsychology. *Journal of Forensic Neuropsychology, 4* (3).

Bush, S. S., & Martin, T. A. (guest editors) (2006). Ethical controversies in neuropsychology. *Applied Neuropsychology, 13* (2).

Deaton, A. V., & Hanson, S. (guest editors) (1996). Special issue on ethics and rehabilitation psychology. Exploring the issues. *Rehabilitation Psychology, 41* (1).

Journal of Head Trauma Rehabilitation (1997). Vol. *12* (1).

McCaffrey, R. J. (guest editor) (2005). Third party observers. *Journal of Forensic Neuropsychology, 4* (2).

Position Papers

American Academy of Clinical Neuropsychology (1999). Policy on the use of non-doctoral-level personnel in conducting clinical neuropsychological evaluations. *Clinical Neuropsychologists, 13* (4), 385.

American Academy of Clinical Neuropsychology (2001). Policy statement on the presence of third party observers in neuropsychological assessment. *Clinical Neuropsychologist, 15*, 433–39.

American Academy of Clinical Neuropsychology (2003). Official position of the American Academy of Clinical Neuropsychology on ethical complaints made against clinical neuropsychologists during adversarial proceedings. *Clinical Neuropsychologist, 17* (4), 443–45.

American Academy of Clinical Neuropsychology (2004). Official position of the American Academy of Clinical Neuropsychology on the role of neuropsychologists in the clinical use of fMRI. *Clinical Neuropsychologist, 18,* 349–51.

American Medical Association, Council on Ethical and Judicial Affairs (1999). *Code of Medical Ethics: Current Opinions with Annotations. 100. Patient-Physician Relationships in the Context of Work-Related and Independent Medical Examinations.* Washington, DC: AMA.

American Psychological Association (1991). *Guidelines for providers of services to ethnic, linguistic, and culturally diverse populations.* Washington, DC: APA.

American Psychological Association (1993). Record keeping guidelines. *American Psychologist, 48,* 984–86.

American Psychological Association (1999). Test security: Protecting the integrity of tests. *American Psychologist, 54,* 1078.

American Psychological Association (2006). Record keeping guidelines. September 2006 draft. Retrieved January 10, 2007, from www.apa.org/practice/recordkeeping.html.

American Psychological Association, Ethics Committee (1998). Services by telephone, teleconferencing, and Internet: A statement by the Ethics Committee of the American Psychological Association. *American Psychologist, 53,* 979.

Bush, S. S., Barth, J. T., Pliskin, N. H., Arffa, S., Axelrod, B. N., Blackburn, L. A., Faust, D., Fisher, J. M., Harley, J. P., Heilbronner, R. L., Larrabee, G. J., Ricker, J. H., & Silver, C. H. (National Academy of Neuropsychology, Policy & Planning Committee) (2005). Independent and court-ordered forensic neuropsychological examinations: Official statement of the National Academy of Neuropsychology. *Archives of Clinical Neuropsychology, 20* (8), 997–1007. Available online at www.nanonline.org/paio/IME.shtm.

Bush, S. S., Ruff, R. M., Tröster, A. I., Barth, J. T., Koffler, S. P., Pliskin, N. H., Reynolds, C. R., & Silver, C. H. (National Academy of Neuropsychology, Policy & Planning Committee) (2005). Symptom validity assessment: Practice issues and medical necessity. Official position of the National Academy of Neuropsychology. *Archives of Clinical Neuropsychology, 20* (4), 419–26.

Committee on Ethical Guidelines for Forensic Psychologists (1991). Specialty guidelines for forensic psychologists. *Law and Human Behavior, 15* (6), 655–65.

Committee on the Revision of the Ethical Guidelines for Forensic Psychologists (2005). Specialty guidelines for forensic psychology. Available online at www.ap-ls.org/links (SGFP version 2.0).

Department of Veterans Affairs (1997). *Assessment of competency and capacity of the older adult: A practice guideline for psychologists* (publication no. PB97-147904). Milwaukee, WI: National Center for Cost Containment.

Division 40 of the American Psychological Association (1989). Definition of a clinical neuropsychologist. *Clinical Neuropsychologist, 3*, 22.

Harcourt Assessment (2003). *HIPAA position statement.* Retrieved April 5, 2004, from marketplace.psychcorp.com.

Johnson-Green, D., & the NAN Policy & Planning Committee (2005). Informed consent in clinical neuropsychology practice: Official statement of the National Academy of Neuropsychology. *Archives of Clinical Neuropsychology, 20*, 335–40.

National Academy of Neuropsychology (2000). Presence of third party observers during neuropsychological testing: Official statement of the National Academy of Neuropsychology. *Archives of Clinical Neuropsychology, 15* (5), 379–80.

National Academy of Neuropsychology (2000). Test security: Official statement of the National Academy of Neuropsychology. *Archives of Clinical Neuropsychology, 15* (5), 383–86.

National Academy of Neuropsychology (2000). The use of neuropsychology test technicians in clinical practice: Official statement of the National Academy of Neuropsychology. *Archives of Clinical Neuropsychology, 15* (5), 381–82.

National Academy of Neuropsychology (2002). *Cognitive rehabilitation: Official statement of the National Academy of Neuropsychology.* Available online at www.nanonline.org/paio/cogrehab.shtm.

National Academy of Neuropsychology, Policy & Planning Committee (2000). Handling requests to release test data, recording and/or reproductions of test data. *Official statement of the National Academy of Neuropsychology*. Available online at www.nanonline.org/paio/secappend.shtm.

National Academy of Neuropsychology, Policy & Planning Committee (2003). Test Security: An update. *Official statement of the National Academy of Neuropsychology*. Available online at www.nanonline.org/paio/security_update.shtm.

Psychological Corporation (2004). Releasing test materials: Position of the Psychological Corporation. *Bulletin of the National Academy of Neuropsychology, 19* (1), 1–8.

Puente, A. E., Adams, R., Barr, W. B., Bush, S. S., Ruff, R. M., & Barth, J. T. (Academy of Neuropsychology, Policy & Planning Committee) (2006). The use, education, training, and supervision of neuropsychological test technicians (psychometrists) in clinical practice. Official statement of the National Academy of Neuropsychology. *Archives of Clinical Neuropsychology, 21,* 837–39.

Silver, C. H., Blackburn, L. B., Arffa, S., Barth, J. T., Bush, S. S., Koffler, S. P., Pliskin, N. H., Reynolds, C. R., Ruff, R. M., Tröster, A. I., Moser, R. S., & Elliott, R. W. (NAN Policy & Planning Committee) (2006). The importance of neuropsychological assessment for the evaluation of childhood learning disorders. Official statement of the National Academy of Neuropsychology. *Archives of Clinical Neuropsychology, 21,* 741–44.

Topics and Settings

APA ETHICS CODE REVISION

Adams, K. M. (2003). It's a whole new world: Or is it? Reflections on the new APA Ethics Code. *Newsletter 40, 21* (1), 5–6 & 18.

Bush, S. S. (2005). Differences between the 1992 and 2002 APA Ethics Codes: A brief overview. In S. S. Bush (ed.), *A casebook of ethical challenges in neuropsychology* (pp. 1–8). New York: Psychology Press.

Bush, S., & Macciocchi, S. (2003). The 2002 APA Ethics Code: Select changes relevant to neuropsychology. *Bulletin of the National Academy of Neuropsychology, 18* (2), 1–2 & 7–8.

Bush, S., Goldberg, A., & Johnson-Greene, D. (2003). Rehabilitation psychology ethics: Understanding and applying the 2002 APA Ethics Code. *Rehabilitation Psychology News, 30* (4), 13–15.

Erard, R. E. (2004). Release of test data under the 2002 Ethics Code and the HIPAA privacy rule. *Journal of Personality Assessment, 82*(1), 23–30.

Knapp, S., & VandeCreek, L. (2003). An overview of the major changes in the 2002 APA Ethics Code. *Professional Psychology: Research and Practice, 34* (3), 301–8.

Knapp, S., & Vandecreek, L. (2004). A principle-based analysis of the 2002 American Psychological Association ethics code. *Psychotherapy: Theory, Research, Practice, Training, 41* (3), 247–54.

ASSESSMENT

Anderson, R. M. Jr., & Shields, H. (1998). Ethical issues in neuropsychological assessment. In R. M. Anderson, Jr., T. L. Needels, & H. V. Hall (eds.), *Avoiding ethical misconduct in psychology specialty areas* (pp. 131–41). Springfield, IL: Charles C. Thomas.

Binder, L. M., & Thompson, L. L. (1995). The ethics code and neuropsychological assessment practices. *Archives of Clinical Neuropsychology, 10* (1), 27–46.

Fisher, J. M., Johnson-Greene, D., & Barth, J. T. (2002). Examination, diagnosis, and interventions in clinical neuropsychology in general and with special populations: An overview. In S. S. Bush & M. L. Drexler (eds.), *Ethical issues in clinical neuropsychology* (pp. 3–22). Lisse, Netherlands: Swets & Zeitlinger.

Messick, S. (1999). Test validity and the ethics of assessment. In D. N. Bersoff (ed.), *Ethical conflicts in psychology*, 2nd ed. (pp. 285–86). Washington, DC: APA.

Thompson, L. L. (2002). Ethical issues in interpreting and explaining neuropsychological assessment results. In S. S. Bush & M. L. Drexler (eds.),

Ethical issues in clinical neuropsychology (pp. 51–72). Lisse, Netherlands: Swets & Zeitlinger.

Wong, T. M. (2006). Ethical controversies in neuropsychological test selection, administration, and interpretation. *Applied Neuropsychology, 13*, 68–76.

COLLEAGUES

Deidan, C., & Bush, S. (2002). Addressing perceived ethical violations by colleagues. In S. S. Bush & M. L. Drexler (eds.), *Ethical issues in clinical neuropsychology* (pp. 281–305). Lisse, Netherlands: Swets & Zeitlinger.

Keith-Spiegel, P., & Koocher, G. P. (1998). How to confront an unethical colleague. In G. P. Koocher, J. C. Norcross, & S. S. Hill (eds.), *Psychologists' desk reference*. New York: Oxford University Press.

COMPETENCE (PROFESSIONAL) AND CREDENTIALING

Bornstein, R. A. (1991). Report of the Division 40 Task Force on Education, Accreditation and Credentialing: Recommendations for education and training of nondoctoral personnel in clinical neuropsychology. *Clinical Neuropsychologist, 5* (1), 20–23.

McSweeny, A. J., & Naugle, R. I. (2002). Competence and appropriate use of neuropsychological assessments and interventions. In S. Bush & M. Drexler (eds.), *Ethical issues in clinical neuropsychology* (pp. 23–37). Lisse, Netherlands: Swets & Zeitlinger.

CONFIDENTIALITY

Bush, S. S., & Martin, T. A. (forthcoming). Confidentiality in neuropsychological practice. In A. M. Horton Jr. & D. Wedding (eds.), *The neuropsychology handbook,* 3rd ed. New York: Springer.

Kerkhoff, T., Babin, P., Bush, S., Goldberg, A., & Hansen, S. (2001). Individual and caregiver rights: Ethical challenges of competency and confidentiality. *Rehabilitation Psychology, 46*, 328 [abstract].

DECISION-MAKING CAPACITY (COMPETENCE)
(ALSO SEE INFORMED CONSENT.)

Appelbaum, P.S. (1998). Missing the boat: Competence and consent in psychiatric research. *American Journal of Psychiatry, 155*, 1486–88.

Appelbaum, P. S., & Grisso, T. (1988). Assessing patient's capacity to consent to treatment. *New England Journal of Medicine, 319*, 1635–38.

Appelbaum, P. S., & Grisso, T. (1995). The MacArthur Treatment Competence Study. I: Mental illness and competence to consent to treatment. *Law and Human Behavior, 19*, 105–26.

Carpenter, W. T., Gold, J. M., Lahti, A. C., Queern, C. A., Conley, R. R., Bartko, J. J., Kovnick, J., & Appelbaum, P. S. (2000). Decisional capacity for informed consent in schizophrenia research. *Archives of General Psychiatry, 57*, 533–38.

DeRenzo, E. G., Conley, R. R., & Love, R. (1998). Assessment of capacity to give consent to research participation: State-of-the-art and beyond. *Journal of Health Care, Law & Policy, 1*, 66–87.

Fowles, G. P., & Fox, B. A. (1995). Competency to consent to treatment and informed consent in neurobehavioral rehabilitation. *Clinical Neuropsychologist, 9*(3), 251–57.

Marson, D. C., Cody, H. A., Ingram, K. K., & Harrell, L. E. (1995). Assessing the competency of patients with Alzheimer's disease under different legal standards. *Archives of Neurology, 52*, 949–54.

Moberg, P. J., & Kriele, K. (2006). Evaluation of competency: Ethical considerations for neuropsychologists. *Applied Neuropsychology, 13*, 101–14.

Rosenthal, M., & Lourie, I. (1996). Ethical issues in the evaluation of competence in persons with acquired brain injuries. *NeuroRehabilitation, 6*, 113–21.

DIVERSITY

Artiola i Fortuny, L., & Mullaney, H.A. (1998). Assessing patients whose language you do not know: Can the absurd be ethical? *Clinical Neuropsychologist, 12* (1), 113–26.

Brickman, A. M., Cabo, R., & Manly, J. J. (2006). Ethical issues in cross-cultural neuropsychology. *Applied Neuropsychology, 13*, 91–100.

Dede, D. E. (2005). Ethical challenges with ethnically and culturally diverse populations in neuropsychology, part I. In S. S. Bush (ed.), *A casebook of ethical challenges in neuropsychology* (pp. 163–69). New York: Psychology Press.

Harris, J. G. (2002). Ethical decision making with individuals of diverse ethnic, cultural, and linguistic backgrounds. In S. S. Bush & M. L. Drexler (eds.), *Ethical issues in clinical neuropsychology* (pp. 223–41). Lisse, Netherlands: Swets & Zeitlinger.

Iverson, G. L. (2000). Neuropsychological evaluations of Asian linguistic minorities in mild head injury litigation. *American Journal of Forensic Psychology, 18* (4), 63–83.

Iverson, G. L., & Slick, D. J. (2003). Ethical issues associated with psychological and neuropsychological assessment of persons from different cultural and linguistic backgrounds. In I. Z. Schultz & D. O. Brady (eds.), *Psychological injuries at trial* (pp. 2066–87). Chicago: American Bar Association.

Manly, J. J., & Jacobs, D. M. (2002). Future directions in neuropsychological assessment with African Americans. In F. R. Ferraro (ed.), *Minority and cross-cultural aspects of neuropsychological assessment* (pp. 79–96). Lisse, Netherlands: Swets & Zeitlinger.

Martin, T. A. (2005). Ethical challenges with ethnically and culturally diverse populations in neuropsychology, part II. In S. S. Bush (ed.), *A casebook of ethical challenges in neuropsychology* (pp. 170–76). New York: Psychology Press.

ENHANCEMENT

Bush, S. S. (2006). Neurocognitive enhancement: Ethical issues for an emerging subspecialty. *Applied Neuropsychology, 13* (2), 125–36.

Chatterjee, A. (2004). Cosmetic neurology: The controversy over enhancing movement, mentation, and mood. *Neurology, 63*, 968–74.

Dees, R. H. (2004). Slippery slopes, wonder drugs, and cosmetic neurology: The neuroethics of enhancement. *Neurology, 63*, 951–52.

Farah, M. J., Illes, J., Cook-Deegan, R., Gardner, H., Kandel, E., King, P., et al. (2004). Neurocognitive enhancement: What can we do and what should we do? *Nature Reviews Neuroscience, 5*, 421–25.

Wolpe, P. R. (2002). Treatment, enhancement, and the ethics of neurotherapeutics. *Brain and Cognition, 50*, 387–95.

ETHICAL CHALLENGES AND ISSUES

Brittain, J. L., Frances, J. P., & Barth, J. T. (1995). Ethical issues and dilemmas in neuropsychological practice reported by ABCN diplomates. *Advances in Medical Psychotherapy, 8*, 1–22.

Bush, S. S., & Martin, T. A. (2006). Introduction to ethical controversies in neuropsychology. *Applied Neuropsychology, 13* (2), 63–67.

Bush, S.S., Grote, C., Johnson-Greene, D., & Macartney-Filgate, M. (2007). A panel interview on the ethical practice of neuropsychology. *Clinical Neuropsychologist*.

ETHICAL DECISION MAKING

Treppa, J. A. (1998). A practitioner's guide to ethical decision-making. In R. M. Anderson Jr., T. L. Needles, & H. V. Hall (Eds.), *Avoiding ethical misconduct in psychology specialty areas*. Springfield, IL: Charles C. Thomas.

FEEDBACK

Pope, K. S. (1992). Responsibilities in providing psychological test feedback to clients. *Psychological Assessment, 4*, 268–71.

FORENSIC ACTIVITIES

Ameis, A., Zasler, N. D., Martelli, M. F., & Bush, S. S. (2006). Ethical issues in clinicolegal practice. In N. D. Zasler, D. Katz, & R. Zafonte (eds.), *Brain injury medicine: Principles and practice* (pp. 1163–82). New York: Demos Medical Publishing.

Bush, S.S. (2005). Introduction to ethical issues in forensic neuropsychology. *Journal of Forensic Neuropsychology, 4* (3), 1–9.

Bush, S. S. (2005). Ethical challenges in forensic neuropsychology: Introduction. In S. S. Bush (ed.), *A casebook of ethical challenges in neuropsychology* (pp. 10–14). New York: Psychology Press.

Bush, S. S., & Lees-Haley, P. R. (2005). Threats to the validity of forensic neuropsychological data: Ethical considerations. *Journal of Forensic Neuropsychology, 4* (3), 45–66.

Connell, M., & Koocher, G. P. (2003). HIPAA and forensic practice. *American Psychology Law Society News*, 23 (2), 16–19.

Crown, B. M., Fingerhut, H. S., & Lowenthal, S. J. (2003). Conflicts of interest and other pitfalls for the expert witness. In A. M. Horton Jr. & L. C. Hartlage (eds.), *Handbook of forensic neuropsychology* (pp. 383–421). New York: Springer.

Denney, R. L. (2005). Ethical challenges in forensic neuropsychology, part I. In S. S. Bush (ed.), *A casebook of ethical challenges in neuropsychology* (pp. 15–22). New York: Psychology Press.

Greenberg, L. R., & Gould, J. W. (2001). The treating expert: A hybrid role with firm boundaries. *Professional Psychology: Research and Practice, 32* (5), 469–78.

Greenberg, S., & Shuman, D. (1997). Irreconcilable conflict between therapeutic and forensic roles. *Professional Psychology: Research and Practice, 28*, 50–57.

Grote, C. L. (2005). Ethical challenges in forensic neuropsychology, part II. In S. S. Bush (ed.), *A casebook of ethical challenges in neuropsychology* (pp. 23–29). New York: Psychology Press.

Grote, C. L. (2005). Ethical practice of forensic neuropsychology. In G. J. Larrabee (ed.), *Forensic neuropsychology: A scientific approach* (pp. 92–114). New York: Oxford University Press.

Grote, C. L., & Parsons, T. D. (2005). Threats to the livelihood of the forensic neuropsychological practice: Avoiding ethical misconduct. *Journal of Forensic Neuropsychology, 4* (3), 79–93.

Grote, C. L., Lewin, J. L., Sweet, J. J., & van Gorp, W. G. (2000). Responses to perceived unethical practices in clinical neuropsychology: Ethical and legal considerations. *Clinical Neuropsychologist, 14* (1), 119–34.

Guilmette, T.J., & Hagan, L.D. (1997). Ethical considerations in forensic neuro-psychological consultation. *Clinical Neuropsychologist, 11* (3), 287–90.

Hartlage, L. C. (2003). Neuropsychology in the courtroom. In A. M. Horton Jr. & L. C. Hartlage (eds.), *Handbook of forensic neuropsychology* (pp. 315–33). New York: Springer.

Iverson, G. L. (2000). Dual relationships in psycholegal evaluations: Treating psychologists service as expert witnesses. *American Journal of Forensic Psychology, 18* (2), 79–87.

Johnson-Greene, D., & Bechtold, K. T. (2002). Ethical considerations for peer review in forensic neuropsychology. *Clinical Neuropsychologist, 16* (1), 97–104.

Lees-Haley, P. (1999). Commentary on Sweet and Moulthrop's debiasing procedures. *Journal of Forensic Neuropsychology, 1*, 43–57.

Lees-Haley, P. R., & Cohen, L. J. (1999). The neuropsychologist as expert witness: Toward credible science in the courtroom. In J. J. Sweet (ed.), *Forensic neuropsychology: Fundamentals and practice* (pp. 443–68). Lisse, Netherlands: Swets & Zeitlinger.

Macartney-Filgate, M. S., & Snow, W. G. (2004). The practitioner as expert witness. In. D. R. Evans (ed.), *The law, standards, and ethics in the practice of psychology,* 2nd ed. Toronto: Emond Montgomery.

Malina, A. C., Nelson, N. W., & Sweet, J. J. (2005). Framing the relationships in forensic neuropsychology: Ethical issues. *Journal of Forensic Neuropsychology, 4* (3), 21–44.

Martelli, M. F., & Zasler, N. D. (2001). Promoting ethics and objectivity in medicolegal contexts: Recommendations for experts. In R. B. Weiner (ed.), *Pain management: A practical guide for clinicians,* 6th ed. (pp. 895–907). Boca Raton, FL: St. Lucie Press.

Martelli, M. F., Bush, S. S., & Zasler, N. D. (2003). Identifying, avoiding, and addressing ethical misconduct in neuropsychological medicolegal practice. *International Journal of Forensic Psychology, 1* (1), 26–44.

Martelli, M., Zasler, N., & Grayson, R. (1999). Ethical considerations in medicolegal evaluations of neurologic injury and impairment following acquired brain injury. *NeuroRehabilitation: An Interdisciplinary Journal, 13*, 45–66.

Martelli, M. F., Zasler, N. D. & Grayson, R. (1999). Ethical considerations in impairment and disability evaluations following acquired brain injury. In R. V. May & M. F. Martelli (eds.), *Guide to functional capacity evaluation with impairment rating applications.* Richmond: NADEP.

Martelli, M. F., Zasler, N. D., & Johnson-Greene, D. (2001). Promoting ethical and objective practice in the medicolegal arena of disability evaluation. *Physical Medicine and Rehabilitation Clinics of North America, 12* (3), 571–84.

Macartney-Filgate, M., & Snow, W. (2000). Forensic assessments and professional relations. *Division 40 Newsletter, 18*(2), 28–31.

Morgan, J. E., & Bush, S. S. (2005). Anticipating forensic involvement: Ethical considerations for clinical neuropsychologists. *Journal of Forensic Neuropsychology, 4* (3), 11–20.

Roper, B. L. (2005). Ethical challenges in forensic neuropsychology, part IV. In S. S. Bush (ed.), *A casebook of ethical challenges in neuropsychology* (pp. 39–50). New York: Psychology Press.

Shuman, D. W., & Greenberg, S. A. (1998, winter). The role of ethical norms in the admissibility of expert testimony. *Judge's Journal*, 5–9 & 42.

Simon, R. I. (1996). Legal and ethical issues. In J. R. Rundell et al. (eds.), *The American Psychiatric Press textbook of consultation-liaison psychiatry*. Washington, DC: American Psychiatric Press.

Slick, D. J., & Iverson, G. L. (2003). Ethical issues in forensic neuropsychological assessment. In I. Z. Schultz & D. O. Brady (eds.), *Psychological injuries at trial*, (pp. 2014–34). Chicago: American Bar Association.

Strasburger, H., Gutheil, T., & Brodsky, B. (1997). On wearing two hats: Role conflict in serving as both psychotherapist and expert witness. *American Journal of Psychiatry, 154*, 448–56.

Sweet, J. J. (2005). Ethical challenges in forensic neuropsychology, part V. In S. S. Bush (ed.), *A casebook of ethical challenges in neuropsychology* (pp. 15–22). New York: Psychology Press.

Sweet, J. J., & Moulthrop, M. A. (1999). Self-examination questions as a means of identifying bias in adversarial assessments. *Journal of Forensic Neuropsychology, 1* (1), 73–88.

Sweet, J. J., & Moulthrop, M. (1999). Response to Lees-Haley's commentary: Debiasing techniques cannot be completely curative. *Journal of Forensic Neuropsychology, 1*, 49–57.

Sweet, J. J., Grote, C., & van Gorp, W. G. (2002). Ethical issues in forensic neuropsychology. In S. S. Bush & M. L. Drexler (eds.), *Ethical issues in clinical neuropsychology* (pp. 103–33). Lisse, Netherlands: Swets & Zeitlinger.

Tranel, D. (2000). Commentary on Lees-Haley and Courtney: There is a need for reform. *Neuropsychology Review, 10* (3), 177–78.

van Gorp, W. G., & Kalechstein, A. (2005). Threats to the validity of the interpretation and conveyance of forensic neuropsychological results. *Journal of Forensic Neuropsychology, 4* (3), 67–77.

van Gorp, W., & McMullen, W. (1997). Potential sources of bias in forensic neuropsychological evaluations. *Clinical Neuropsychologist, 11*, 180–87.

Youngjohn, J., Spector, J., & Mapou, R. (1998). Failure to assess motivation, need to consider psychiatric disturbance, and absence of objectively verified physical pathology: Some common pitfalls in the practice of forensic neuropsychology. *Clinical Neuropsychologist, 12*, 233–36.

GERIATRIC

Bush, S. S., & Martin, T. A. (2005). Ethical issues in geriatric neuropsychology. In S. S. Bush & T. A. Martin (eds.), *Geriatric neuropsychology: Practice essentials* (pp. 507–36). New York: Psychology Press.

McSweeny, A.J. (2005). Ethical challenges in geriatric neuropsychology, part I. In S.S. Bush (Ed.), *A casebook of ethical challenges in neuropsychology* (pp. 147–52). New York: Psychology Press.

Morgan, J. (2002). Ethical issues in the practice of geriatric neuropsychology. In S.S. Bush & M. L. Drexler (eds.), *Ethical issues in clinical neuropsychology* (pp. 87–101). Lisse, Netherlands: Swets & Zeitlinger.

Morgan, J. E. (2005). Ethical challenges in geriatric neuropsychology, part II. In S. S. Bush (ed.), *A casebook of ethical challenges in neuropsychology* (pp. 153–58). New York: Psychology Press.

INFORMED CONSENT

Appelbaum, P. S. (1998). Missing the boat: Competence and consent in psychiatric research. *American Journal of Psychiatry, 155*, 1486–88.

Appelbaum, P. S., & Grisso, T. (1988). Assessing patient's capacity to consent to treatment. *New England Journal of Medicine, 319*, 1635–38.

Appelbaum, P. S., & Grisso, T. (1995). The MacArthur Treatment Competence Study. I: Mental illness and competence to consent to treatment. *Law and Human Behavior, 19,* 105–26.

Appelbaum, P. S., Roth, L. H., & Lidz, C. W. (1982). The therapeutic misconception: Informed consent in psychiatric research. *International Journal of Law and Psychiatry, 5,* 319–29.

Argarwal, M. R., Ferran, J., Ost, K., & Wilson, K. (1996). Ethics of informed consent in dementia research-the debate continues. *International Journal of Geriatric Psychiatry, 11,* 801–6.

Benson, P. R., Roth, L. H., & Winslade, W. J. (1985). Informed consent in psychiatric research: Preliminary findings from an ongoing investigation. *Social Science & Medicine, 20* (12), 1331–41.

Bush, S., & Sandberg, M. (2001). Utilizing "assent" to determine "consent": Proposed ethical revisions and their implications for TBI rehabilitation. *Archives of Clinical Neuropsychology, 16,* 807 [abstract].

Carpenter, W. T., Gold, J. M., Lahti, A. C., Queern, C. A., Conley, R. R., Bartko, J. J., Kovnick, J., & Appelbaum, P. S. (2000). Decisional capacity for informed consent in schizophrenia research. *Archives of General Psychiatry, 57,* 533–38.

DeRenzo, E. G., Conley, R. R., & Love, R. (1998). Assessment of capacity to give consent to research participation: State-of-the-art and beyond. *Journal of Health Care, Law & Policy, 1,* 66–87.

Fowles, G. P., & Fox, B. A. (1995). Competency to consent to treatment and informed consent in neurobehavioral rehabilitation. *Clinical Neuropsychologist, 9*(3), 251–57.

Franzi, C., Orgren, R. A., & Rozance, C. (1995). Informed consent by proxy: A dilemma in long term care research. *Clinical Gerontologist, 15,* 23–34.

Johnson-Greene, D., Hardy-Morais, C., Adams, K. M., Hardy, C., & Bergloff, P. (1997). Informed consent and neuropsychological assessment: Ethical considerations and proposed guidelines. *Clinical Psychologist, 11* (4), 454–60.

Macciocchi, S.N. (2001). Informed consent and neuropsychological assessment. *Newsletter 40,* Winter/Spring, 34–36.

Wichman, A., & Sandler, A. (1995). Research in subjects involving dementia and other cognitive impairments: Experience at the NIH, and some unresolved ethical considerations. *Neurology, 45,* 1777–78.

Also see Decision-Making Capacity (Competence)

MEDICAL SETTINGS

Bush, S.S. (forthcoming). Legal and ethical considerations in rehabilitation and health assessment. In E. Mpofu & T. Oakland (eds.), *Assessment in Rehabilitation and Health.* Boston: Allyn & Bacon.

Pinkston, J. B. (2005). Ethical challenges in neuropsychology in medical settings, part I. In S. S. Bush (ed.), *A casebook of ethical challenges in neuropsychology* (pp. 65–70). New York: Psychology Press.

Wilde, E. A. (2005). Ethical challenges in neuropsychology in medical settings, part II. In S. S. Bush (ed.), *A casebook of ethical challenges in neuropsychology* (pp. 71–80). New York: Psychology Press.

Wilde, E., Bush, S., & Zeifert, P. (2002). Ethical issues in neuropsychology in medical settings. In S. Bush & M. L. Drexler (eds.), *Ethical issues in clinical neuropsychology* (pp. 195–221). Lisse, Netherlands: Swets & Zeitlinger.

Wong, T. M. (1998). Ethical issues in the evaluation and treatment of brain injury. In R. M. Anderson Jr., T. L. Needles, & H. V. Hall (eds.), *Avoiding ethical misconduct in psychology specialty areas* (pp. 187–200). Springfield, IL: Charles C. Thomas.

PAIN

Martelli, M. F. (2005). Ethical challenges in the neuropsychology of pain, part I. In S. S. Bush (ed.), *A casebook of ethical challenges in neuropsychology* (pp. 113–23). New York: Psychology Press.

Nicholson, K. (2005). Ethical challenges in the neuropsychology of pain, part II. In S. S. Bush (ed.), *A casebook of ethical challenges in neuropsychology* (pp. 124–30). New York: Psychology Press.

PEDIATRIC

Fennell, E. B. (2002). Ethical issues in pediatric neuropsychology. In S. S. Bush & M. L. Drexler (eds.), *Ethical issues in clinical neuropsychology* (pp. 75–86). Lisse, Netherlands: Swets & Zeitlinger.

Fennell, E. B. (2005). Ethical challenges in pediatric neuropsychology, part I. In S.S. Bush (Ed.), *A casebook of ethical challenges in neuropsychology* (pp. 133-136). New York: Psychology Press.

Goldberg, A. L. (2005). Ethical challenges in pediatric neuropsychology, part II. In S. S. Bush (ed.), *A casebook of ethical challenges in neuropsychology* (pp. 137–44). New York: Psychology Press.

Latham, P. S., & Latham, P. H. (1998). Selected legal issues. In C. E. Coffey & R. A. Brumback (eds.), *Textbook of child neuropsychiatry* (pp. 1491–506). Washington, DC: APA.

Woody, R. H. (1989). Public policy and legal issues for clinical child neuropsychology. In C. R. Reynolds & E. Fletcher-Janzen (eds.), *Handbook of clinical child neuropsychology: Critical issues in neuropsychology*. New York: Plenum Press.

PSYCHIATRIC

Gur, R. C., Moberg, P. J., & Wolpe, P. R. (2002). Ethical issues in neuropsychology in psychiatric settings. In S. S. Bush & M. L. Drexler (eds.), *Ethical issues in clinical neuropsychology* (pp. 165–93). Lisse, Netherlands: Swets & Zeitlinger.

Moberg, P.J. (2005). Ethical challenges in neuropsychology in psychiatric settings, part I. In S. S. Bush (ed.), *A casebook of ethical challenges in neuropsychology* (pp. 83–88). New York: Psychology Press.

Yozawitz, A. (2005). Ethical challenges in neuropsychology in psychiatric settings, part II. In S. S. Bush (ed.), *A casebook of ethical challenges in neuropsychology* (pp. 89–94). New York: Psychology Press.

RAW TEST DATA, RECORDS, AND PATIENT INFORMATION

Barth, J.T. (2000). Commentary on "Disclosure of tests and raw test data to the courts" by Paul Lees-Haley and John Courtney. *Neuropsychology Review, 10* (3), 179–80.

Behnke, S. (2003). Release of test data and APA's new Ethics Code. *Monitor on Psychology, 34* (7), 70–72.

Bush, S. S., & Martin, T. A. (2006). The ethical and clinical practice of disclosing raw test data: Addressing the ongoing debate. *Applied Neuropsychology, 13*, 125–36.

Bush, S., Behnke, S., Chadda, R., Johnson-Greene, D., Sims, D., & Stein, S. (2004). The revised Ethics Code: Release of test information to non-psychologists. *Clinical Neuropsychologist, 18*, 201–2 [abstract].

Erard, R. E. (2004). "A raw deal" reheated: Reply to comments by Rogers, Fischer, Smith and Evans. *Journal of Personality Assessment, 82* (1), 44–47.

Fisher, C. B. (2003). Test data standard most notable change in new APA ethics code. *National Psychologist*, January/February, 12–13.

Freides, D. (1993). Proposed standard of professional practice: Neuropsychological reports display all quantitative data. *Clinical Neuropsychologist, 7*, 234–35.

Freides, D. (1995). Interpretations are more benign than data. *Clinical Neuropsychologist, 9*, 248.

Holloway, J. D. (2003). A stop-gap in the flow of sensitive patient information. *Monitor on Psychology, 34* (3), 28.

Lees-Haley, P. R., & Courtney, J. C. (2000). Disclosure of tests and raw test data to the courts: A need for reform. *Neuropsychology Review, 10* (3), 169–75.

Lees-Haley, P. R., & Courtney, J. C. (2000). Reply to the commentary on "Disclosure of tests and raw test data to the courts." *Neuropsychology Review, 10* (3), 181–82.

Naugle, R. I. & McSweeny, A. J. (1995). On the practice of routinely appending neuropsychological data to reports. *Clinical Neuropsychologist, 9* (3), 245–47.

Naugle, R. I. & McSweeny, A. J. (1996). More thoughts on the practice of routinely appending raw data to reports: Response to Freides and Matarazzo. *Clinical Neuropsychologist, 10*, 313–14.

Piazza, N. J., & Baruth, N. E. (1990). Patient record guidelines. *Journal of Counseling & Development, 68*, 313–16.

Rapp, D. L., & Ferber, P. S. (2003). To release, or not to release raw test data, that is the question. In A. M. Horton Jr. & L. C. Hartlage (eds.), *Handbook of forensic neuropsychology* (pp. 337–68). New York: Springer.

Rapp, D. L., Ferber, P. S., & Bush, S. S. (in press). Unresolved issues about release of test data and test materials. In A. M. Horton Jr. & L.C.

Hartlage (eds.), *Handbook of forensic neuropsychology,* 2nd ed. New York: Springer.

Rogers, R. (2004). APA 2002 ethic, amphibology, and the release of psychological test records: A counterperspective to Erard. *Journal of Personality Assessment, 82* (1), 31–34.

Shapiro, D. L. (2000). Commentary: Disclosure of tests and raw data to the courts. *Neuropsychology Review, 10* (3), 175–76.

Sweet, J. (1990). Further consideration of ethics in psychological testing: A broader perspective on releasing records. *Illinois Psychologist, 28,* 5–9.

REHABILITATION (BRAIN INJURY)

Banja, J. D. (1996). Ethics, values, and world culture: The impact on rehabilitation. *Disability Rehabilitation, 18* (6), 279–84.

Banja, J. (1999). Patient advocacy at risk: Ethical, legal and political dimensions of adverse reimbursement practices in brain injury rehabilitation in the US. *Brain Injury, 13*(10), 745–58.

Banja, J., & Johnston, M. V. (1994). Outcomes evaluation in TBI rehabilitation. Part III: Ethical perspectives and social policy. *Archives of Physical Medicine and Rehabilitation, 75*(12), SC19-26; discussion SC 27–28.

Banja, J. D., Adler, R. K., & Stringer, A. Y. (1996). Ethical dimensions of caring for defiant patients: A case study. *Journal of Head Trauma Rehabilitation, 11* (6), 93–97.

Berube, J. E. (2000). The auto choice reform act. *Journal of Head Trauma Rehabilitation, 15*(4), 1063–67.

Bush, S. (2000). Ethical issues in neuropsychological life and death decisions: A rehabilitation case study. *Archives of Clinical Neuropsychology, 16,* 620 [abstract].

DeLuca, J. (2005). Ethical challenges in neuropsychology in rehabilitation settings, part I. In S. S. Bush (ed.), *A casebook of ethical challenges in neuropsychology* (pp. 97–103). New York: Psychology Press.

Hanson, S., Guenther, R., Kerkhoff, T., & Liss, M. (2000). Ethics: Historical foundations, basic principles and contemporary issues. In R. Frank & T.

Elliott (eds.), *Handbook of rehabilitation psychology* (pp. 629–43). Washington, DC: APA.

Johnson-Greene, D. (2005). Ethical challenges in neuropsychology in rehabilitation settings, part II. In S.S. Bush (ed.), *A casebook of ethical challenges in neuropsychology* (pp. 104–10). New York: Psychology Press.

Juriga, M., & Bush, S. (2002). Attention to biomedical ethics may improve rehabilitation outcome: A case illustration. *Rehabilitation Psychology, 47*, 374–75 [abstract].

Malec, J. F. (1993). Ethics in brain injury rehabilitation: existential choices among western cultural beliefs. *Brain Injury, 7*(5), 383–400.

Malec, J. F. (1996). Ethical conflict resolution based on an ethics of relationships for brain injury rehabilitation. *Brain Injury, 10*(11), 781–95.

Rosenthal, M. (1996). 1995 Sheldon Berrol, MD Senior Lectureship: The Ethics and efficacy of traumatic brain injury rehabilitation-myths, measurements, and meaning. *Journal of Head Trauma Rehabilitation, 11*(4), 88–95.

Sim, J. (1998). Respect for autonomy: Issues in neurological rehabilitation. *Clinical Rehabilitation, 12* (1), 3–10.

Swiercinsky, D. P. (2002). Ethical issues in neuropsychological rehabilitation. In S. S. Bush & M. L. Drexler (eds.), *Ethical issues in clinical neuropsychology* (pp. 201–8). Lisse, Netherlands: Swets & Zeitlinger.

Wilson, B. A. (1997). Cognitive rehabilitation: How it is and how it might be. *Journal of the International Neuropsychological Society, 3*(5), 487–96.

RESEARCH

Roberts, L. W., & Roberts, B. R. (1999). Psychiatric research ethics: An overview of evolving guidelines and current ethical dilemmas in the study of mental illness. *Biological Psychiatry, 46*, 1025–38.

Thompson, L. L. (2005). Ethical challenges in neuropsychological research, part I. In S. S. Bush (ed.), *A casebook of ethical challenges in neuropsychology* (pp. 201–8). New York: Psychology Press.

van Gorp, W. G. (2005). Ethical challenges in neuropsychological research, part II. In S. S. Bush (ed.), *A casebook of ethical challenges in neuropsychology* (pp. 209–12). New York: Psychology Press.

SPORTS

Echemendia, R. J., & Parker, E. (1998). Ethical issues in the neuropsychological assessment of athletes. In J. Bailes, M. Lovell, & J. Maroon (eds.), *Sports related concussion and nervous system injuries*. St. Louis, MO: Quality Medical Publishers.

Parker, E. J., Echemendia, R. J., & Milhouse, C. (2004). Ethical issues in the evaluation of athletes. In M. Lovell, R. Echemendia, J. Barth, & M. Collins (eds.), *Traumatic brain injury in sports: An international neuropsychological perspective* (pp. 467–77). Lisse, Netherlands: Swets & Zeitlinger Publishers.

SYMPTOM VALIDITY ASSESSMENT

Bush, S. S. (forthcoming). Ethical implications for the assessment of symptom validity. *Praxis der Rechtspsychologie*.

Cox, D. R. (2005). Ethical challenges in the determination of response validity in neuropsychology, part I. In S. S. Bush (ed.), *A casebook of ethical challenges in neuropsychology* (pp. 229–37). New York: Psychology Press.

Crouch, J. A. (2005). Ethical challenges in the determination of response validity in neuropsychology, part II. In S. S. Bush (ed.), *A casebook of ethical challenges in neuropsychology* (pp. 238–49). New York: Psychology Press.

Iverson, G. L. (2006). Ethical issues associated with the assessment of exaggeration, poor effort, and malingering. *Applied Neuropsychology, 13*, 77–90.

TECHNICIANS

DeLuca, J. W. (1989) Neuropsychology technicians in clinical practice: Precedents, rationale and current deployment. *Clinical Neuropsychologist, 3*(1), 3–21.

TECHNOLOGY

Ackerman, R. J., & Banks, M. E. (1990). Computers and ethical treatment for brain-injured patients. *Social Science Computer Review, 8* (1), 83–95.

Browndyke, J.N. (2005). Ethical challenges with the use of information technology and telecommunications in neuropsychology, part I. In S. S. Bush (ed.), *A casebook of ethical challenges in neuropsychology* (pp. 179–89). New York: Psychology Press.

Bush, S. (2002). The interface of information technology and rehabilitation psychology: Ethical issues and recommendations. *Rehabilitation Psychology, 47*, 356 [abstract].

Bush, S., Naugle, R., & Johnson-Greene, D. (2002). The interface of information technology and neuropsychology: Ethical issues and recommendations. *Clinical Neuropsychologist, 16* (4), 536–47.

Matthews, C. G., Harley, J. P., & Malec, J. F. (1991). Guidelines for computer-assisted neuropsychological rehabilitation and cognitive remediation. *Clinical Neuropsychologist, 5* (1), 3–19.

McMinn, M. R., Ellens, B. M., & Soref, E. (1999). Ethical perspectives and practice behaviors involving computer-based test interpretation. *Assessment, 6*, 71–77.

Naglieri, J. A., Drasgow, F., Schmit, M., et al. (2004). Psychological testing on the internet: New problems, old issues. *American Psychologist, 59*, 150–62.

Rizzo, A., Schultheis, M. T., & Rothbaum, B. O. (2002). Ethical issues for the use of virtual reality in the psychological sciences. In S. S. Bush & M. L. Drexler (eds.), *Ethical issues in clinical neuropsychology* (pp. 243–79). Lisse, Netherlands: Swets & Zeitlinger.

Schatz, P. (2005). Ethical challenges with the use of information technology and telecommunications in neuropsychology, part II. In S. S. Bush (ed.), *A casebook of ethical challenges in neuropsychology* (pp. 190–98). New York: Psychology Press.

TEST CONSTRUCTION

Anderson, R. M. Jr., & Palozzi, A. M. (2002). Ethical issues in test construction, selection, and security. In S. S. Bush & M. L. Drexler (eds.), *Ethical issues in clinical neuropsychology* (pp. 39–50). Lisse, Netherlands: Swets & Zeitlinger.

Golden, C.J. (2005). Ethical challenges in neuropsychological test development, part I. In S. S. Bush (ed.), *A casebook of ethical challenges in neuropsychology* (pp. 215–20). New York: Psychology Press.

Sivan, A. B. (2005). Ethical challenges in neuropsychological test development, part II. In S. S. Bush (ed.), *A casebook of ethical challenges in neuropsychology* (pp. 221–26). New York: Psychology Press.

THIRD-PARTY OBSERVERS

Binder, L. M., & Johnson-Greene, D. (1995). Observer effects on neuropsychological performance: A case report. *Clinical Neuropsychologist, 9*, 74–78.

Blase, J. J. (2003). Trained third-party presence during forensic neuropsychological evaluations. In A. M. Horton Jr. & L. C. Hartlage (eds.), *Handbook of forensic neuropsychology* (pp. 369–82). New York: Springer.

Butler, J., & Baumeister, R. F. (1998). The trouble with friendly faces: Skilled performance with a supportive audience. *Journal of Personality and Social Psychology, 75*, 1213–30.

Constantinou, M., & McCaffrey, R. J. (2003). The effects of 3rd party observation: When the observer is a video camera. *Archives of Clinical Neuropsychology, 18*, 788–89 [abstract].

Constantinou, M., Ashendorf, L., & McCaffrey, R. J. (2002). When the 3rd party observer of a neuropsychological evaluation is an audio-recorder. *Clinical Neuropsychologist, 16* (3), 407–12.

Constantinou, M., Ashendorf, L., & McCaffrey, R.J. (2005). Effects of a third party observer during neuropsychological assessment: When the observer is a video camera. *Journal of Forensic Neuropsychology, 4*, 39–48.

Duff, K., & Fisher, J. M. (2005). Ethical dilemmas with third party observers. *Journal of Forensic Neuropsychology, 4*, 65–82.

Gavett, B. E., Lynch, J. K., & McCaffrey, R. J. (2003). Third party observers: The effect size is greater than you might think. *Archives of Clinical Neuropsychology, 18*, 789–90 [abstract].

Gavett, B. E., Lynch, J. K., & McCaffrey, R. J. (2005). Third party observers: The effect size is greater than you might think. *Journal of Forensic Neuropsychology, 4*, 49–64.

Kehrer, C., Sanchez, P., Habif, U., Rosenbaum, J. G., & Townes, B. (2000). Effects of a significant-other observer on neuropsychological test performance. *Clinical Neuropsychologist, 14*, 67–71.

LaCalle, J. (1987). Forensic psychological evaluations through an interpreter: Legal and ethical issues. *American Journal of Forensic Psychology, 5*, 29–43.

Lynch, J. K. (2003). The effect of an observer on neuropsychological test performance following TBI. *Archives of Clinical Neuropsychology, 18*, 791 [abstract].

Lynch, J. K. (2005). Effect of a third party observer on neuropsychological test performance following closed head injury. *Journal of Forensic Neuropsychology, 4*, 17–26.

McCaffrey, R. J. (2005). Some final thoughts and comments regarding the issue of third party observers. *Journal of Forensic Neuropsychology, 4*, 83–91.

McCaffrey, R. J., Fisher, J. M., Gold, B. A., & Lynch, J. K. (1996). Presence of third parties during neuropsychological evaluation: Who is evaluating whom? *Clinical Neuropsychologist, 10*(4), 435–49.

McCaffrey, R. J., Lynch, J. K., & Yantz, C. L. (2005). Third party observers: Why all the fuss? *Journal of Forensic Neuropsychology, 4*, 1–16.

McSweeny, A. J., Becker, B. C., Naugle, R. I., Snow, W. G., Binder, L. M., & Thompson, L. L. (1998). Ethical issues related to presence of third party observers in clinical neuropsychological evaluations. *Clinical Neuropsychologist, 12* (4), 552–60.

Yantz, C. L., & McCaffrey, R. J. (2006). Effects of a supervisor's observation on memory test performance of the examinee: Third party observer effect confirmed. *Journal of Forensic Neuropsychology, 4*, 27–38.

References

Ackerman, R. J., & Banks, M. E. (1990). Computers and ethical treatment for brain-injured patients. *Social Science Computer Review, 8*, 83–95.

American Academy of Clinical Neuropsychology (2001). Policy statement on the presence of third party observers in neuropsychological assessment. *Clinical Neuropsychologist, 15*, 433–39.

American Academy of Clinical Neuropsychology (2003). Official position of the American Academy of Clinical Neuropsychology on ethical complaints made against clinical neuropsychologists during adversarial proceedings. *Clinical Neuropsychologist, 17* (4), 443–45.

American Educational Research Association, American Psychological Association, & National Council on Measurement in Education (1999). *Standards for educational and psychological testing.* Washington, DC: Author.

American Psychological Association (1992). Ethical principles of psychologists and code of conduct. *American Psychologist, 47*, 1597–611.

American Psychological Association (1993). Record keeping guidelines. *American Psychologist, 48*, 984–86.

American Psychological Association (2002). Ethical principles of psychologists and code of conduct. *American Psychologist, 57* (12), 1060–73.

American Psychological Association (2006). Record keeping guidelines. September 2006 draft. Retrieved January 10, 2007, from ww.apa.org/practice/recordkeeping.html.

American Psychological Association, Division of Neuropsychology (1989). Definition of a clinical neuropsychologist. *Clinical Neuropsychologist, 3*, 22.

Americans with Disabilities Act of 1990, Public Law Number 101-336, 104 Stat. 328.

Anderson, Jr., R. M., & Palozzi, A. M. (2002). Ethical issues in test construction, selection, and security. In S. S. Bush & M. L. Drexler (eds.), *Ethical issues in clinical neuropsychology* (pp. 39–50). Lisse, Netherlands: Swets & Zeitlinger Publishers.

Artiola i Fortuny, L., & Mullaney, H. A. (1998). Assessing patients whose language you do not know: Can the absurd be ethical? *Clinical Neuropsychologist, 12* (1), 113–26.

Association of State and Provincial Psychology Boards (2005). *ASPPB code of conduct*. Retrieved January 28, 2005, from www.asppb.org.

Ball, K., Berch, D. B., Helmers, K. F., Jobe, J. B., Leveck, M. D., Marsiske, M., et al. (2002). Effects of cognitive training interventions with older adults. *Journal of the American Medical Association, 288* (18), 2271–81.

Banja, J. D., ed. (1989). Ethical and legal issues (special issue). *Journal of Head Trauma Rehabilitation, 4* (1).

Barsky, A. E., & Gould, J. W. (2002). *Clinicians in court: A guide to subpoenas, depositions, testifying, and everything else you need to know.* New York: Guilford Press.

Beauchamp, T. L., & Childress, J. F. (2001). *Principles of biomedical ethics* (5th ed.). New York: Oxford University Press.

Behnke, S. H., Perlin, M. L., & Bernstein, M. (2003). *The essentials of New York mental health law: A straightforward guide for clinicians of all disciplines.* New York: Norton.

Binder, L. M., & Thompson, L. L. (1995). The ethics code and neuropsychological assessment practices. *Archives of Clinical Neuropsychology, 10,* 27–46.

Bornstein, R. A. (1991). Report of the Division 40 Task Force on Education, Accreditation and Credentialing: Recommendations for education and training of nondoctoral personnel in clinical neuropsychology. *Clinical Neuropsychologist, 5,* 20–23.

Brickman, A. M., Cabo, R., & Manly, J. J. (2006). Ethical issues in cross-cultural neuropsychology. *Applied Neuropsychology, 13,* 91–100.

Brittain, J. L., Frances, J. P., & Barth, J. T. (1995). Ethical issues and dilemmas in neuropsychological practice reported by ABCN diplomates. *Advances in Medical Psychotherapy, 8*, 1–22.

Browndyke, J. N. (2005). Ethical challenges with the use of information technology and telecommunications in neuropsychology, part I. In S. S. Bush (ed.), *A casebook of ethical challenges in neuropsychology* (pp. 179–89). New York: Psychology Press.

Bush, S. S., ed. (2005a). *A casebook of ethical challenges in neuropsychology.* New York: Psychology Press.

Bush, S. S. (2005b). Ethical issues in forensic neuropsychology: Introduction. *Journal of Forensic Neuropsychology, 4* (3), 1–9.

Bush, S. S. (2005c). Ethical issues in forensic neuropsychology. *Journal of Forensic Neuropsychology, 4* (3).

Bush, S. S. (2005d). Differences between the 1992 and 2002 APA Ethics Codes: A brief overview. In S. S. Bush (ed.), *A casebook of ethical challenges in neuropsychology* (pp. 1–8). New York: Psychology Press.

Bush, S. S. (2006). Neurocognitive enhancement: Ethical issues for an emerging subspecialty. *Applied Neuropsychology, 13* (2), 125–36.

Bush, S. S. (in press). Ethical implications for the assessment of symptom validity. *Praxis der Rechtspsychologie.*

Bush, S. S., & Drexler, M. L., eds. (2002). *Ethical issues in clinical neuropsychology.* Lisse, Netherlands: Swets & Zeitlinger Publishers.

Bush, S. S., & Lees-Haley, P. R. (2005). Threats to the validity of forensic neuropsychological data: Ethical considerations. *Journal of Forensic Neuropsychology, 4* (3), 45–66.

Bush, S., & Martin, T. (2004). *Balancing bioethical principles in computer-based memory treatment.* Poster presentation, 9th International Conference on Alzheimer's Disease and Related Disorders. Philadelphia, PA, July 18.

Bush, S .S., & Martin, T. A. (2005a). Ethical issues in geriatric neuropsychology. In S.S. Bush & T.A. Martin (eds.), *Geriatric neuropsychology: Practice essentials* (pp. 507–36). New York: Psychology Press.

Bush, S. S., & Martin, T. A., eds. (2005b). *Geriatric neuropsychology: Practice essentials.* New York: Psychology Press.

Bush, S. S., & Martin, T. A. (2006a). Introduction to ethical controversies in neuropsychology. *Applied Neuropsychology, 13* (2), 63–67.

Bush, S. S., & Martin, T. A. (2006b). Ethical controversies in neuropsychology. *Applied Neuropsychology, 13* (2).

Bush, S. S., & Martin, T. A. (2006c). The ethical and clinical practice of disclosing raw test data: Addressing the ongoing debate. *Applied Neuropsychology, 13,* 125–136.

Bush, S. S., & Martin, T.A. (in press). Confidentiality in neuropsychological practice. In A. M. Horton Jr. & D. Wedding (eds.), *The neuropsychology handbook,* 3rd ed. New York: Springer.

Bush, S. S., Barth, J. T., Pliskin, N. H., Arffa, S., Axelrod, B. N., Blackburn, L. A., Faust, D., Fisher, J. M., Harley, J. P., Heilbronner, R. L., Larrabee, G. J., Ricker, J. H., & Silver, C. H. (National Academy of Neuropsychology Policy & Planning Committee) (2005a). Independent and court-ordered forensic neuropsychological examinations: Official statement of the National Academy of Neuropsychology. *Archives of Clinical Neuropsychology, 20* (8), 997–1007. Available online at www.nanonline.org/paio/IME.shtm.

Bush, S. S., Connell, M. A., & Denney, R. L. (2006). *Ethical practice in forensic psychology: A systematic model for decision making.* Washington, DC: American Psychological Association.

Bush, S. S., Grote, C., Johnson-Greene, D., & Macartney-Filgate, M. (in press). A panel interview on the ethical practice of neuropsychology. *Clinical Neuropsychologist, 21.*

Bush, S., Naugle, R., & Johnson-Greene, D. (2002). The interface of information technology and neuropsychology: Ethical issues and recommendations. *Clinical Neuropsychologist, 16* (4), 536–47.

Bush, S. S., Ruff, R. M., Tröster, A. I., Barth, J. T., Koffler, S. P., Pliskin, N. H., Reynolds, C. R., & Silver, C. H. (National Academy of Neuropsychology Policy & Planning Committee) (2005b). Symptom validity assessment: Practice issues and medical necessity. Official position of the National Academy of Neuropsychology. *Archives of Clinical Neuropsychology, 20* (4), 419–26.

Canadian Psychological Association (2000). *Canadian code of ethics for psychologists,* 3rd ed. Ottawa, Ontario: CPA.

Caplan, B., & Shechter, J. (2005). Test accommodations in geriatric neuropsychology. In S. S. Bush & T. A. Martin (eds.), *Geriatric neuropsychology: Practice essentials* (pp. 97–114). New York: Psychology Press.

Carpenter v. Superior Court of Alameda County (Yamaha Motor Corp., USA), Cal.App.4th (2006).

Cicerone, K. D., Dahlberg, C., Malec, J. F., Langenbahn, D. M., Felicetti, T., Kneipp, S., Ellmo, W., Kalmar, K., Giacino, J. T., Harley, J. P., Laatsch, L., Morse, P. A., & Catanese, J. (2005). Evidence-based cognitive rehabilitation: Updated review of the literature from 1998 through 2002. *Archives of Physical Medicine and Rehabilitation, 86,* 1681–92.

Committee on the Revision of the Ethical Guidelines for Forensic Psychologists (2005). *Specialty guidelines for forensic psychology.* Retrieved January 10, 2006, from www.ap-ls.org/links (SGFP version 2.0).

Connell, M., & Koocher, G.P. (2003). HIPAA and forensic practice. *American Psychology Law Society News, 23,* 16–19.

Constantinou, M., Ashendorf, L., & McCaffrey, R. J. (2002). When the 3rd party observer of a neuropsychological evaluation is an audio-recorder. *Clinical Neuropsychologist, 16* (3), 407–12.

Constantinou, M., Ashendorf, L., & McCaffrey, R. J. (2005). Effects of a third party observer during neuropsychological assessment: When the observer is a video camera. *Journal of Forensic Neuropsychology, 4,* 39–48.

Daubert v. Merrell Dow Pharmaceuticals, Inc., 509 U.S. 579 (1993).

Dede, D. E. (2005). Ethical challenges with ethnically and culturally diverse populations in neuropsychology, part I. In S. S. Bush (ed.), *A casebook of ethical challenges in neuropsychology* (pp. 163–69). New York: Psychology Press.

Deidan, C., & Bush, S. (2002). Addressing perceived ethical violations by colleagues. In S. S. Bush & M. L. Drexler (eds.), *Ethical issues in clinical neuropsychology* (pp. 281–305). Lisse, Netherlands: Swets & Zeitlinger.

Detroit Edison Co. v. NLRB, 440 U.S. 301 (1979).

Doukas, D., & McCullough, L. (1991). The values history: The evaluation of the patient's values and advance directives. *Journal of Family Practice, 32,* 145–50.

Echemendia, R. J., ed. (2006). *Sports neuropsychology: Assessment and management of traumatic brain injury.* New York: Guilford Press.

Eisenstadt v. Baird, 405 U.S. 438. (1972).

Erard, R. E. (2004). Release of test data under the 2002 Ethics Code and the HIPAA privacy rule. *Journal of Personality Assessment, 82* (1), 23–30.

Fisher, J. M., Johnson-Greene, D., & Barth, J. T. (2002). Examination, diagnosis, and interventions in clinical neuropsychology in general and with special populations: An overview. In S. S. Bush & M. L. Drexler (eds.), *Ethical issues in clinical neuropsychology* (pp. 3–22). Lisse, Netherlands: Swets & Zeitlinger.

Grote, C. L. (2005). Ethical practice of forensic neuropsychology. In G. J. Larrabee (ed.), *Forensic neuropsychology: A scientific approach* (pp. 92–114). New York: Oxford University Press.

Grote, C. L., Lewin, J. L., Sweet, J. J., & van Gorp, W. G. (2000). Responses to perceived unethical practices in clinical neuropsychology: Ethical and legal considerations. *Clinical Neuropsychologist, 14* (1), 119–34.

Haas, L., & Malouf, J. (2002). *Keeping up the good work: A practitioner's guide to mental health ethics* (3rd ed.). Sarasota, FL: Professional Resource Press.

Iverson, G. L. (2000a). Dual relationships in psycholegal evaluations: Treating psychologists service as expert witnesses. *American Journal of Forensic Psychology, 18* (2), 79–87.

Iverson, G. L. (2000b). Neuropsychological evaluations of Asian linguistic minorities in mild head injury litigation. *American Journal of Forensic Psychology, 18* (4), 63–83.

Iverson, G. L. (2006). Ethical issues associated with the assessment of exaggeration, poor effort, and malingering. *Applied Neuropsychology, 13,* 77–90.

Iverson, G. L., & Slick, D. J. (2003). Ethical issues associated with psychological and neuropsychological assessment of persons from different cultural and linguistic backgrounds. In I. Z. Schultz & D. O. Brady (eds.),

Psychological injuries at trial (pp. 2066–87). Chicago: American Bar Association.

Johnson-Green, D., & the NAN Policy & Planning Committee (2005). Informed consent in clinical neuropsychology practice: Official statement of the National Academy of Neuropsychology. *Archives of Clinical Neuropsychology, 20*, 335–40.

Kitchener, K. S. (2000). *Foundations of ethical practice, research, and teaching.* Mahwah, NJ: Erlbaum.

Knapp, S., & VandeCreek, L. (2003a). *A guide to the 2002 revision of the American Psychological Association's Ethics Code.* Sarasota, FL: Professional Resource Press.

Knapp, S., & VandeCreek, L. (2003b). An overview of the major changes in the 2002 APA Ethics Code. *Professional Psychology: Research and Practice, 34* (3), 301–8.

Knapp, S., & VandeCreek, L. (2006). *Practical ethics for psychologists: A positive approach.* Washington, DC: American Psychological Association.

Koocher, G. P., & Keith-Spiegel, P. (1998). *Ethics in psychology: Professional standards and cases* (2nd ed.). New York: Oxford University Press.

Kramer, A. F., Bherer, L., Colcombe, S. J., Dong,W., & Greenough, W. T. (2004). Environmental influences on cognitive and brain plasticity during aging. *Journal of Gerontology: Medical Sciences, 59A* (9), 940–57.

Larrabee, G. J., ed. (2005). *Forensic neuropsychology: A scientific approach.* New York: Oxford University Press.

Malec, J. F. (1993). Ethics in brain injury rehabilitation: Existential choices among western cultural beliefs. *Brain Injury, 7*, 383–400.

Manly, J. J., & Jacobs, D. M. (2002). Future directions in neuropsychological assessment with African Americans. In F. R. Ferraro (ed.), *Minority and cross-cultural aspects of neuropsychological assessment* (pp. 79–96). Lisse, Netherlands: Swets & Zeitlinger.

Martelli, M. F., Bush, S. S., & Zasler, N. D. (2003). Identifying, avoiding, and addressing ethical misconduct in neuropsychological medicolegal practice. *International Journal of Forensic Psychology, 1*, 26–44.

Martin, T. A. (2005). Ethical challenges with ethnically and culturally diverse populations in neuropsychology, part II. In S. S. Bush (ed.), *A casebook of ethical challenges in neuropsychology* (pp. 170–76). New York: Psychology Press.

McCaffrey, R. J. (guest editor) (2005). Third party observers. *Journal of Forensic Neuropsychology, 4* (2), special issue.

McSweeny, A. J. (2002). The oral examination: Professional and ethical issues. In R. L. Mapou (ed.), *American Academy of Neuropsychology study guide for board certification in clinical neuropsychology* (pp. 68–75). Minneapolis, MN: American Academy of Clinical Neuropsychology.

McSweeny, A. J., & Naugle, R. I. (2002). Competence and appropriate use of neuropsychological assessments and interventions. In S. Bush & M. Drexler (eds.), *Ethical issues in clinical neuropsychology* (pp. 23–37). Lisse, Netherlands: Swets & Zeitlinger Publishers.

Merriam-Webster (1988). *Webster's 9th New Collegiate Dictionary*. Springfield, MA: Merriam-Webster.

Nagy, T. F. (2000). *Ethics in plain English: An illustrative casebook for psychologists*. Washington, DC: American Psychological Association.

National Academy of Neuropsychology (2000). Presence of third party observers during neuropsychological testing: Official statement of the National Academy of Neuropsychology. *Archives of Clinical Neuropsychology, 15* (5), 379–80.

National Academy of Neuropsychology (2001). *NAN Definition of a Clinical Neuropsychologist*. Official Position of the National Academy of Neuropsychology. Boulder, CO: Author. Retrieved 4/17/07 from www.nanonline.org

National Academy of Neuropsychology (2002). *Cognitive rehabilitation: Official statement of the National Academy of Neuropsychology*. Available online at www.nanonline.org/paio/cogrehab.shtm.

National Academy of Neuropsychology, Policy & Planning Committee (2000). Handling requests to release test data, recording and/or reproductions of test data. *Official statement of the National Academy of*

Neuropsychology. Available online at www.nanonline.org/paio/secappend.shtm.

National Academy of Neuropsychology, Policy & Planning Committee (2003b). Test Security: An update. *Official statement of the National Academy of Neuropsychology.* Available online at www.nanonline.org/paio/security_update.shtm.

Parker, E. J., Echemendia, R. J., & Milhouse, C. (2004). Ethical issues in the evaluation of athletes. In M. Lovell, R. Echemendia, J. Barth, & M. Collins (eds.), *Traumatic brain injury in sports: An international neuropsychological perspective* (pp. 467–77). Lisse, Netherlands: Swets & Zeitlinger.

Pope, K. S., & Brown, L. (1996). *Recovered memories of abuse: Assessment, therapy, forensics.* Washington, DC: American Psychological Association.

Pope, K. S. & Vetter, V. A. (1992). Ethical dilemmas encountered by members of the American Psychological Association: A national survey. *American Psychologist, 47*, 397–411.

Powell, M. R., Gfeller, J. D., Hendricks, B. L., & Sharland, M. (2004). Detecting symptom- and test-coached simulators with the Test of Memory Malingering. *Archives of Clinical Neuropsychology, 19* (5), 693–702.

Psychological Corporation (2004). Releasing test materials: Position of the Psychological Corporation. *Bulletin of the National Academy of Neuropsychology, 19* (1), 1–8.

Puente, A. E., Adams, R., Barr, W. B., Bush, S. S., Ruff, R. M., Barth, J. T., Broshek, D., Koffler, S. P., Reynolds, C. R., Silver, C. H., & Tröster, A. I. (National Academy of Neuropsychology, Policy & Planning Committee) (2006). The use, education, training, and supervision of neuropsychological test technicians (psychometrists) in clinical practice. Official statement of the National Academy of Neuropsychology. *Archives of Clinical Neuropsychology, 21*, 837–39.

Rapp, D. L., Ferber, P. S., & Bush, S. S. (in press). Unresolved issues about release of test data and test materials. In A. M. Horton, Jr., & L. C. Hartlage (eds.), *Handbook of Forensic Neuropsychology, 2nd Edition.* New York: Springer Publishing Co.

Rompilla v. Beard, 545 U.S. 374 (2005).

Sbordone, R. J., & Long, C. J., eds. (1996). *Ecological validity of neuropsychological testing.* Delray Beach, FL: CRC Press.

Schatz, P. (2005). Ethical challenges with the use of information technology and telecommunications in neuropsychology, part II. In S. S. Bush (ed.), *A casebook of ethical challenges in neuropsychology* (pp. 190–98). New York: Psychology Press.

Silver, C. H., Blackburn, L. B., Arffa, S., Barth, J. T., Bush, S. S., Koffler, S. P., Pliskin, N. H., Reynolds, C. R., Ruff, R. M., Tröster, A. I., Moser, R. S., & Elliott, R. W. (NAN Policy & Planning Committee) (2006). The importance of neuropsychological assessment for the evaluation of childhood learning disorders. Official statement of the National Academy of Neuropsychology. *Archives of Clinical Neuropsychology, 21,* 741–44.

Smith, T. S., McGuire, J. M., Abbott, D. W., & Blau, B. I. (1991). Clinical ethical decision making: An investigation of the rationales used to justify doing less than one believes on should. *Professional Psychology: Research and Practice, 22,* 235–39.

Smith-Bell, M., & Winslade, W. J. (1999). Privacy, confidentiality, and privilege in psychotherapeutic relationships. In D. N. Bersoff (ed.), *Ethical conflicts in psychology* (2nd ed.) (pp. 151–55). Washington, DC: American Psychological Association.

Sweet, J. J. (2005). Ethical challenges in forensic neuropsychology, part V. In S. S. Bush (ed.), *A casebook of ethical challenges in neuropsychology* (pp. 51–61). New York: Psychology Press.

Sweet, J. J., Grote, C., & van Gorp, W. G. (2002). Ethical issues in forensic neuropsychology. In S. S. Bush & M. L. Drexler (eds.), *Ethical issues in clinical neuropsychology* (pp. 103–33). Lisse, Netherlands: Swets & Zeitlinger.

Sweet, J. J., Peck, E., Abramowitz, C., & Etzweiler, S. (2003a). National Academy of Neuropsychology/Division 40 (American Psychological Association) Practice Survey of Clinical Neuropsychology in the United States, Part I: Practitioner and practice characteristics, professional activities, and time requirements. *Clinical Neuropsychologist, 16,* 109–27.

Sweet, J.J., Peck, E., Abramowitz, C., & Etzweiler, S. (2003b). National Academy of Neuropsychology/Division 40 (American Psychological

Association) Practice Survey of Clinical Neuropsychology in the United States, Part II: Reimbursement experiences, practice economics, billing practices, and incomes. *Archives of Clinical Neuropsychology, 18,* 1–26.

Tarasoff v. Regents of the University of California, 551 P.2d 334 (Cal. 1976).

Thompson, L. L. (2002). Ethical issues in interpreting and explaining neuropsychological assessment results. In S. S. Bush & M. L. Drexler (eds.), *Ethical Issues in Clinical Neuropsychology* (pp. 51–72). Lisse, Netherlands: Swets & Zeitlinger publishers.

U.S. Department of Health and Human Services (2003). Public Law 104-191: Health Insurance Portability and Accountability Act of 1996. Retrieved November 24, 2003 from www.hhs.gov/ocr/hipaa.

Uzzell, B. P. (2000). Neuropsychological rehabilitation. In A.-L. Christensen and B. P. Uzzell (eds.), *International handbook of neuropsychological rehabilitation* (pp. 353–69). New York: Kluwer Academic/Plenum Press.

van Gorp, W. G. (2005). Ethical challenges in neuropsychological research, part II. In S. S. Bush (ed.), *A casebook of ethical challenges in neuropsychology* (pp. 209–12). New York: Psychology Press.

Woody, R. H. (1989). Public policy and legal issues for clinical child neuropsychology. In C. R. Reynolds, & E. Fletcher-Janzen (eds), *Handbook of clinical child neuropsychology: Critical issues in neuropsychology.* New York: Plenum Press.

World Health Organization (2001). *International classification of functioning, disability and health (ICF).* Geneva, Switzerland: Author.

About the Author

Shane S. Bush, Ph.D. is in independent practice on Long Island, New York. He is Clinical Assistant Professor in the Department of Psychiatry and Behavioral Science, School of Medicine, State University of New York at Stony Brook; Associate Professor, Department of Rehabilitation Neuropsychology, Touro College School of Health Sciences; and Instructor of Professional Ethics and Neuropsychology, National Academy of Neuropsychology DistanCE program. He is board certified in clinical neuropsychology and rehabilitation psychology by the American Board of Professional Psychology and is board certified in neuropsychology by the American Board of Professional Neuropsychology. He is a fellow of the American Psychological Association, Division of Neuropsychology, and fellow of the National Academy of Neuropsychology. He is an editorial board member of *Clinical Neuropsychologist*, *Applied Neuropsychology*, and *Archives of Clinical Neuropsychology*. He is coeditor of *Ethical Issues in Clinical Neuropsychology*, editor of *A Casebook of Ethical Challenges in Neuropsychology*, coauthor of *Health Care Ethics for Psychologists: A Casebook*, coauthor of *Ethical Practice in Forensic Psychology: A Systematic Model for Decision Making*, and coeditor of *Geriatric Neuropsychology: Practice Essentials*. He has authored and coauthored articles, chapters, and position papers on ethical and professional issues and has presented on ethical issues at national conferences.